# X-STITCH

Cross-stitch projects to make a statement

**Sarah Fordham**

First published 2013 by
**Guild of Master Craftsman Publications Ltd**
Castle Place, 166 High Street, Lewes,
East Sussex, BN7 1XU

ISBN 978 1 86108 906 9

A catalogue record for this book is available from the British Library.

**Publisher** Jonathan Bailey
**Production Manager** Jim Bulley
**Managing Editor** Gerrie Purcell
**Senior Project Editor** Dominique Page
**Editor** Sarah Hoggett
**Managing Art Editor** Gilda Pacitti
**Designer** Rebecca Mothersole
**Photographers** Rebecca Mothersole and Sarah Fordham
**Illustrators** Peters & Zabransky, Kellie Black and Sarah Fordham

Set in Gibson, Cross Stitch Classic,
Cross Stitch Cursive, Cross Stitch Monogram
Colour origination by GMC Reprographics
Printed and bound in China

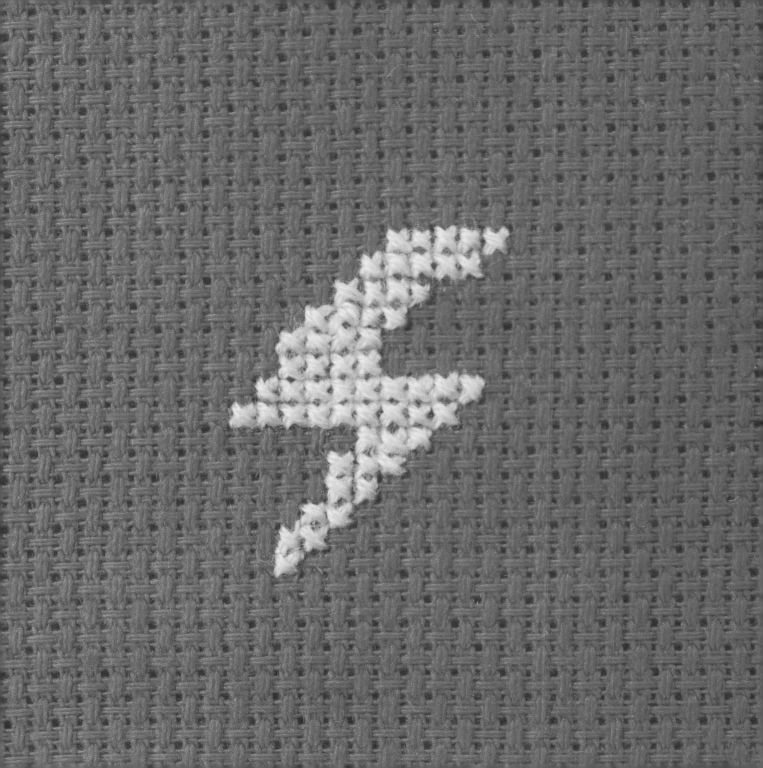

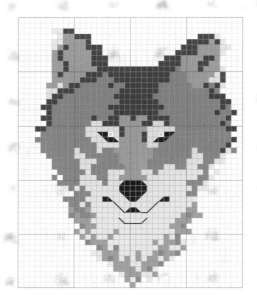

# contents

# INTRODUCTION

I cross stitch pretty much every day. This might sound a little sad, but I really love it! When I first attempted it many years ago, however, I absolutely hated it and thought it seemed too complicated. I have heard many people make the same complaint and hope that the instructions and projects in this book are simple enough to make it a much more fun experience.

As someone who is self-taught, my methods may not be 'text book' or 'professional', but they are simple techniques that I use – and if you know of a better way of doing something or can think up your own techniques, then do whatever you find suits you best. I think it is far more important to have fun with what you make than to worry too much about technique.

In this book I have created 20 projects for you to try out, or simply to look at for some inspiration. Not only are there cross-stitch pictures for you to make, but there are a variety of other contemporary items such as a gadget case, badge and watch strap. Many of the projects involve water-soluble canvas, which is a relatively new product that makes it really easy to produce perfect cross stitches on fabric that isn't evenweave (see page 12), even allowing you to adorn your clothes in cross stitch if you fancy.

I have included a number of cross-stitch charts for you to use in the projects in this book or to use in your own work, and have provided you with the simple tools to go ahead and create your own designs. The beauty of this book is that with each project you have the freedom to choose any cross-stitch design you want: there is no set pattern to follow, only the step-by-step instructions. This way, each of you will be able to create a unique item and will become confident in creating your own cross-stitch work.

I hope that this book will convert a few cross-stitch haters to love it as much as I do – and maybe even inspire you to design some new work of your own.

Sarah

- x -

GETTING STARTED

# HOW TO GO ABOUT CREATING ART

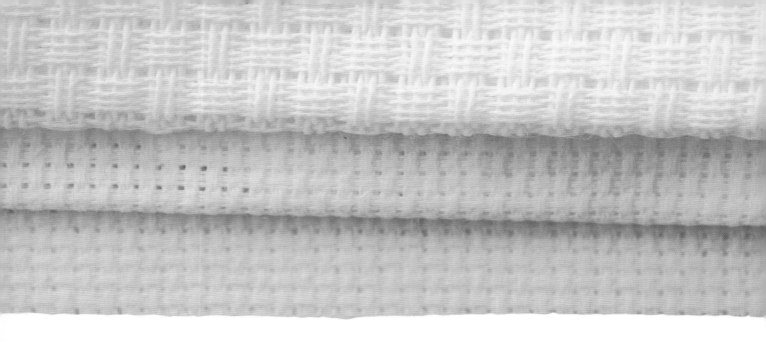

# TOOLS AND MATERIALS

ONE OF THE JOYS OF CROSS STITCH IS THAT YOU NEED RELATIVELY LITTLE IN THE WAY OF SPECIALIST TOOLS AND MATERIALS. THIS SECTION INTRODUCES YOU TO ALL THE BASIC FABRICS, THREADS AND EQUIPMENT.

## Aida

Aida is the name of the fabric used for cross-stitch and needlepoint projects. It is an 'evenweave' fabric. This means that, when you look closely, it is woven to reveal evenly spaced holes – so each stitch is the same size and shape and your finished work looks very neat with minimal effort on your part. Each square on the aida represents where one 'x' or cross stitch will go.

Aida comes in various sizes, and each size will alter the size of your finished work. Each size is named as a 'count'. You can get sizes such as '14-count' or '18-count' and this relates to how many little holes there are per inch (2.5cm); for example, 14-count aida has 14 little holes per inch. The higher the count and the more holes per inch, the smaller your finished motif will be as you have a greater number of stitches to fit in.

I usually work with 14-count aida, but if I want a piece to finish a little smaller I opt for 18-count to scale it down slightly. Get a scrap of each count of aida and try stitching the same little motif on each to compare the finished size.

Do not slip into the habit of buying aida in cream or white all the time – there are so many colours available now that can make your work look so much better. There are even aidas available with pre-printed polka-dot patterns on them, and aida that has metallic thread running through it.

## Binca

Binca is like aida on a large scale. It is often used by children to help them learn to sew, as the holes are so much bigger and easier for them to see. It can be fun to use for large-scale projects. If you'd like to give it a go, I used it for the Pop Art Canvases on pages 106–111.

## Water-soluble canvas

This is one of my new favourite things. Pin or tack it to ordinary fabric and work your cross stitches in exactly the same way as you would with aida. Then wash the piece in hot, soapy water – the canvas will disappear, leaving behind your neatly worked stitches. It allows you a little creative freedom from working on aida all of the time.

## Embroidery thread

There are a few very well known brands of embroidery thread on the market. I do not buy for the brand alone – I choose the shade I am looking for at the time. I even have a lot of embroidery thread that is very cheap and I do not want to discourage you from doing the same. However there is, of course, a difference in quality and you may find that the cheaper threads are more prone to snagging and snapping midway through your stitching. I have even acquired a lot of threads second hand, which is great, but it can be frustrating if you run out of a shade and can't find a matching one again. If you buy your thread new, it will come with a shade number on the label; if you are really organized, try to keep hold of this if you like the colour.

As with the aida, there are so many varieties of thread available now, from neon to metallic. I love metallic thread, although it can be a little frustrating to work with, as it snags and tangles a lot. I find it easier if I keep my thread much shorter than I would normally and ensure that the thread on each stitch is pulled a little tighter.

Apart from fabric and threads, there are other sewing accessories that will come in very handy. See overleaf for my suggestions. Look out for quirky vintage or novelty sewing accessories to perk up your sewing box.

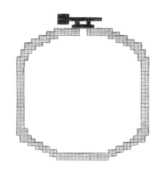

## Needles

As unprofessional as it may sound, I do not buy any fancy needles. I tend to use whatever I can get my hands on at the time. Ideally, though, I don't like using a needle that is too sharp and I like the 'eye' to be a good size for easy threading, and not so big that it will distort any of the holes in your aida as you thread it though.

## Embroidery hoops

Hoops are typically used to hold your aida taut while you work, but they can also act as a decorative frame to complete it. I prefer to stitch without a frame – I find I can work a lot faster.

## Scissors

I use a small pair of scissors for snipping my threads. (Quirky bird-shaped scissors like the ones I use are not essential, of course!) I also have a large pair of scissors for cutting fabric, and a pair of pinking shears for creating a zig-zag edge to reduce fraying or just for decorative purposes. If you're planning to make paper patterns, keep a pair of scissors just for cutting paper; if you use your best fabric scissors for this, they'll blunt really quickly.

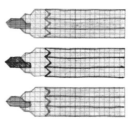

## Pins

All sewing boxes should have a stash of pins. You never know when you may need them, and you will certainly require them for some of the projects in this book. Add a novelty pin cushion to the mix.

## Graph paper and coloured pencils

If you wish to design your own cross-stitch charts, you will need to get hold of some graph paper or use the paper that comes with this book (see pages 145–9). Use coloured pencils to doodle your designs onto the grid. You can even purchase graph-paper sketchbooks – why not carry one in your bag and doodle ideas on the go?

## Thread holders

If, unlike me, you like to keep things organized you can purchase various things to wrap your thread around to keep it tidy and prevent it from becoming tangled. I have a plastic horse-head tidy from DMC Threads, which has several holes dotted around the edge that allow me to thread my thread through and keep it neat. You can also get things such as little cards to wrap your thread around, or perhaps you could even make your own.

## Tape measure and ruler

These are essentials in any sewing kit, as you will need to take measurements for sewing projects or use your tape measure to work out how large a design will be when finished. The ruler can come in handy when working your designs onto graph paper, to help you find the centre point.

## Sewing box

You will need a box to keep all of this equipment in. For a long time I had all of my threads shoved into an old shoe box, but I am now the proud owner of a novelty house-shaped sewing box. I love it to bits and it is huge so I can fit everything in there. The downside is that I am still a messy pig.

## Thimble

A thimble may sound somewhat old fashioned, but let me warn you – cross stitch is a dangerous game! I do not use a thimble, but as a result I am covered in scratches and have a little hole mark in my ring finger from where I repeatedly push my needle onto it. I have also been known to get so close to my work that I scratch my face with my needle. Try not to be as foolish as me!

# HOW TO CROSS STITCH

WHILE ALL THE PROJECTS IN THIS BOOK ARE BASED ON CROSS STITCH, THERE ARE A FEW OTHER STITCHES THAT YOU WILL NEED TO LEARN.

WHEN IT COMES TO EMBROIDERY, I AM SURE EVERYONE HAS THEIR OWN TECHNIQUES AND METHODS, EVEN WHEN IT COMES TO THE SILLIEST LITTLE DETAILS. I AM GOING TO EXPLAIN MY OWN WAY OF WORKING, BUT IF YOU HAVE BEEN TOLD ANOTHER WAY, OR ARE HAPPIER DOING THINGS IN A STYLE YOU ALREADY FEEL CONFIDENT IN, THEN PLEASE CONTINUE TO DO SO.

## Starting off

Grab a skein of embroidery thread. Find the loose end of thread, pull until you have about a forearm's length of thread free and snip it off. If you look closely, you will see that your thread is made up of six tiny strands. I like to use two strands in my work, but some people prefer to use three. This is all personal preference. I would suggest using two for the time being, or experimenting with both on a scrap of aida.

Carefully pull two (or three) strands of thread away and thread your needle. At the other end, you're faced with an option: to knot or not to knot the end of your thread. For a long time, I was perfectly happy putting a tiny knot at the end of my thread, until I realized that many other people don't bother; now I rarely knot the end of my thread. If you put a knot in, you run a tiny risk of it creating a bit of a 'bump' in your finished piece.

As an alternative to making a knot, I just leave the end of my thread loose. As I make my first stitch, I leave about ¾in (2cm) of thread loose at the back of my work. As I stitch, this usually gets caught up with my other stitches.

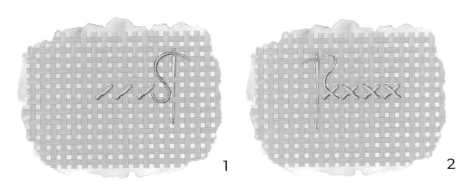

1

2

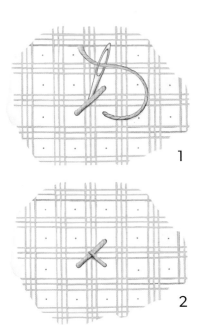

1

2

## Cross stitch

I hate to point out the obvious, but 'cross stitch' is exactly that – stitches that resemble a little 'x' shape. Each stitch is worked in two parts – first, a diagonal stitch in one direction, then another worked on top of it in the opposite direction. On aida evenweave fabric, you bring your needle up through one of the tiny holes, then bring it across the 'square' in the fabric, and diagonally down into the next hole. I like to work from top right, down to the bottom left hole, but it really doesn't matter which way you wish to work so long as every stitch looks the same – with every stitch on the bottom running at the same angle, and every stitch on top at the same angle. This will make your finished piece look neat.

## Half cross stitch

This stitch is just half of one completed cross stitch (see first illustration, above). When working large areas of the same colour, it can be a good idea to work all of the first diagonal 'half stitches' first, before returning to complete the 'x' stitch. Some people like to work all of their cross stitch in this way, by filling most of their work with half stitches and then completing it. It can make you feel as if you are completing your work a little faster!

## Three-quarter stitch

When you are reading a cross-stitch chart and encounter a square that is only half coloured in and resembles a triangle, you do not need to complete a full cross stitch. Make the first half of the cross stitch and bring your needle up through the aida to begin your final stitch – but instead of pushing it down into the opposite hole, push it through the middle of the square in the canvas, so that you are just skimming past the middle of the first stitch. Your stitch will now only take up half of the square in the aida, just like the triangle on your chart.

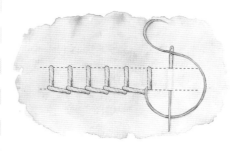

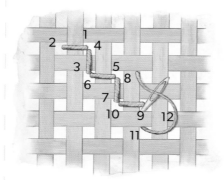

## Running stitch

This stitch is as easy as pie and is probably the simplest stitch around. Simply bring your needle up through your fabric and then, leaving a slight space, take it back down again to form a straight line. All the stitches should be of equal length if you want your work to look well finished, and each stitch is straight.

You could play around with grouping the stitches together to form a block of colour (as above) or experiment with different lengths of stitches.

## Backstitch

Backstitch is very similar to running stitch. Instead of running all of your stitches forward and leaving a space between each one, once you have completed one stitch, imagine where your next stitch would be; bring your needle up at the end of this imaginary stitch, then take it back down next to where your last stitch ended. You should have two stitches sitting right next to each other, either in a straight line or at angles as shown above.

## Blanket stitch

Blanket stitch probably looks far more complicated than it really is. It is a really nice way to give your finished work a pretty edge. Bring the needle up through the aida at the edge of your work. Leaving a slight space as you would when working a running stitch (see far left), push the needle back down through the aida – but instead of pulling your thread through tightly, leave a little loop. Bring your needle back up through this loop and pull gently. Repeat by bringing your needle through your aida from the back of your work to the front, leaving an equal space again, and threading your needle through the loop of thread at the top again. You should now have a series of straight stitches parallel to each other, with a piece of thread along the bottom linking them together.

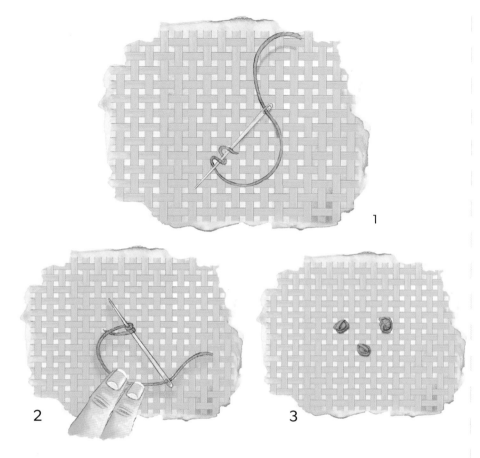

1

2

3

## Finishing off

When I have finished a piece of work, I simply pass my needle and thread through the back of a few stitches and snip it off. This means that you haven't had to create a knot, which can be messy and result in creating a bumpy finished piece – especially if you are using a lot of different colours in a small space. By passing your thread through the back of a few stitches on the reverse of your work, you are keeping that little piece of thread neatly held in place. If you were to just cut your thread at the back, you would run the risk of your stitches coming loose.

With small pieces of work, you probably won't see any creases in the aida, but for larger-scale work it is always a nice idea to give it a gentle press under an iron. To be on the safe side, place a piece of clean thin fabric or a sheet of greaseproof paper over your work to protect it from the iron just in case it is dirty.

## French knot

A lot of cross-stitch charts use French knots to act as 'eyes' on characters and motifs. You will need to use both hands when completing this stitch, so it can be a bit fiddly. Bring your needle up through your work in the exact spot you would like your French knot to be placed. Wrap your thread around the needle once or twice, then push the needle back through your canvas in roughly the same hole that you brought it up through. While doing so, make sure your threads are pulled taut so that the knot you create is as neat as possible.

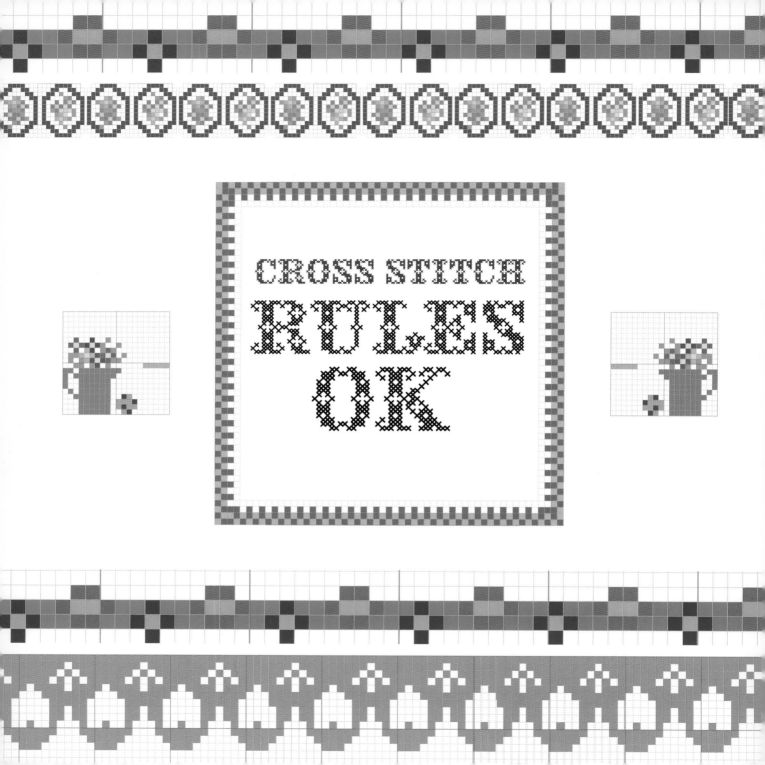

# UNDERSTANDING THE CHARTS

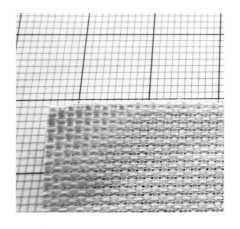

If you use the graph paper supplied with this book (see pages 145–9), you will notice that the size of squares on the graph corresponds with the size of 'squares' on your aida of the same count. Each 'square' of aida fabric has a hole at each corner. Work each cross stitch so that it covers each of these squares.

Cross-stitch charts can consist of black-and-white symbols on a grid, with each symbol relating to a different-coloured thread, or they can be coloured squares on a grid. The latter style of chart is a much easier to follow, as you don't have to keep referring to a key to work out which symbol relates to which colour. On pages 26–47 there are a number of themed cross-stitch charts either for you to use or to inspire your own designs. Within these charts, you will find the motifs that are used in the projects. Feel free to copy them or to use entirely different designs. However, if you are new to cross stitch, I recommend you choose some of the really small motifs to practise with on a scrap of aida.

I tend to work with whichever threads are lurking in my sewing box, so you could do the same. If, however, you're shopping for threads to use with these charts, you could always take this book with you, so that you can compare the chart colours with the shades of embroidery thread available.

**Get creative**

You do not have to use the designs exactly as they appear in this book. Many of the designs can be broken down – look at the borders on pages 32–3, for example, and how all these designs are made up of much smaller motifs that you could use on their own.

# DESIGNING CROSS STITCH

FOR ME, THIS IS THE BEST BIT. AS MUCH AS I ENJOY THE ACTUAL STITCHING OF THE WORK, I REALLY ENJOY COMING UP WITH DESIGNS – I HOPE THAT YOU WILL, TOO.

Cross-stitch designs can be done in a number of ways, but the most popular method is to use graph paper. Since each square represents a single cross stitch, you can colour in the graph paper with your chosen design and work from that. What many books lack is graph paper that allows you to work to scale. On pages 145–9, you will find graph paper that is exactly the same size as the aida you will be using – which means that the size of your design on the paper will be exactly the same size as on your aida! This has been a real help for me when making my own work.

On the facing page are the stages I go through when designing a cross-stitch motif.

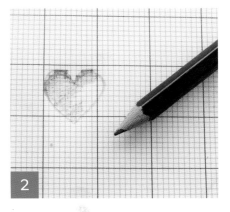

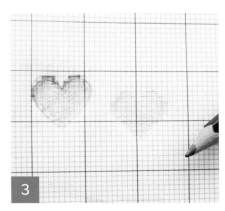

Each square represents one stitch.

1 To use the graph paper, you could just dive straight in and colour the individual blocks, but sometimes I find it easier to sketch your design really roughly onto the paper, as here.

2 I then try to make the rough sketch fit the grid better by drawing over the rough lines and following the squares in the paper.

3 Once I have a rough sketch, I copy it out again so that I can see it more clearly. Then I can have fun playing with colour. If you want your image to have a smoother outline, use three-quarter stitches to form a little 'triangle' instead of a full cross stitch. These help to add a little shape to your work.

### Get inspired

You can use the graph paper to copy out some of my charts and alter them – maybe you would like to see how they look if the colours were changed, or perhaps you want to add or remove some of the stitches I have suggested.

You can also use the graph paper to draw around a frame or object that you would like your work to sit in, to get an idea of how much space you have to stitch your work in. This may seem really basic, but why overcomplicate things?

# THE IDEAS FACTORY

CROSS-STITCH
CHARTS

# Lumber Jack

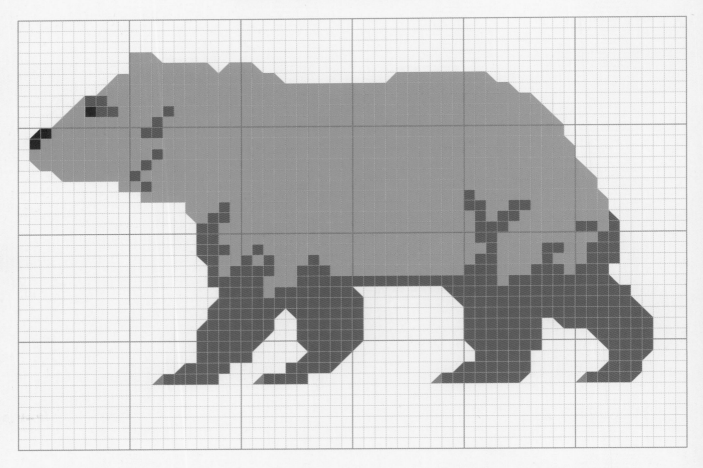

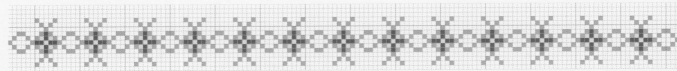

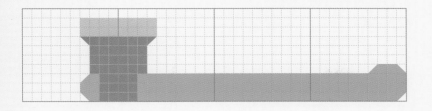

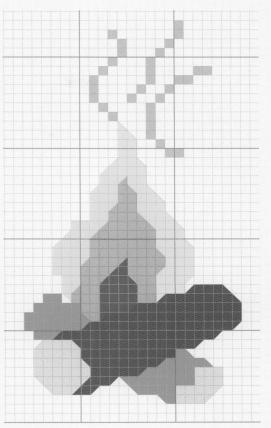

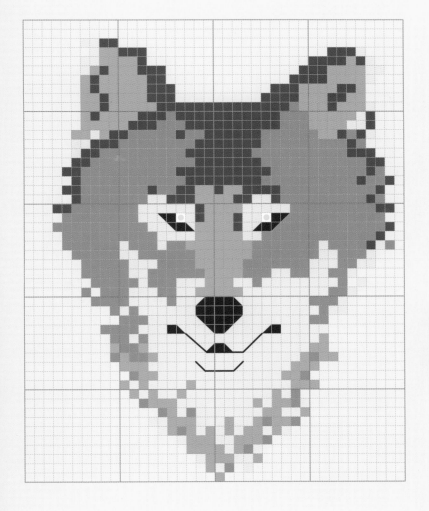

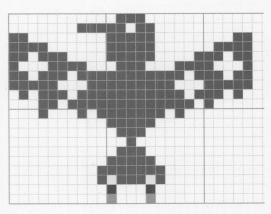

*Grizzly bears and log fires; these designs look good worked on sandy brown and natural-coloured aida.*

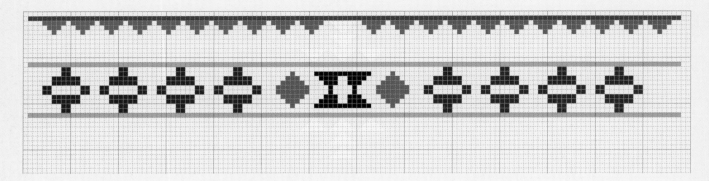

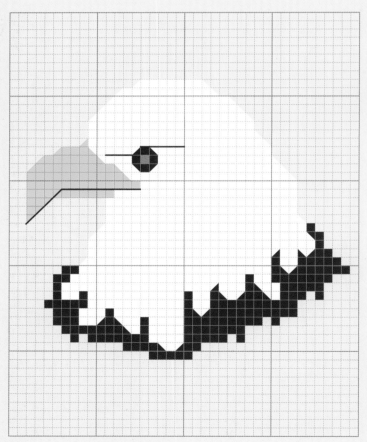

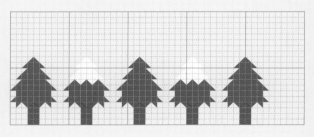

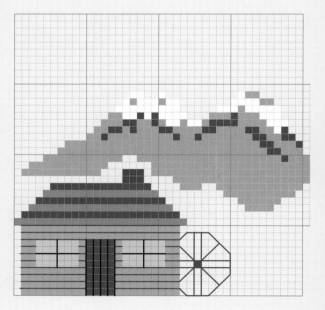

# Tattoo

Too scared to get the real thing?
Or perhaps you're an ink addict?
Stitch these tattoo themes to adorn your walls.

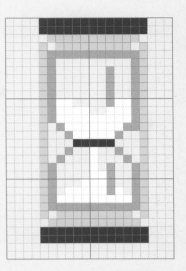

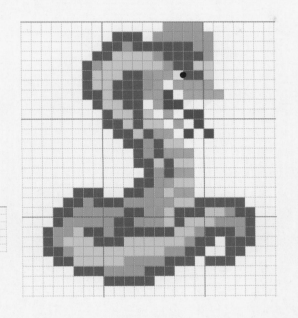

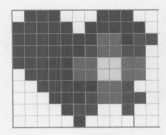

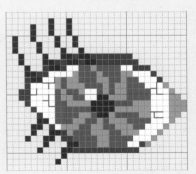

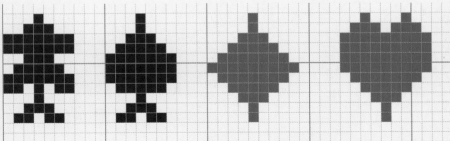

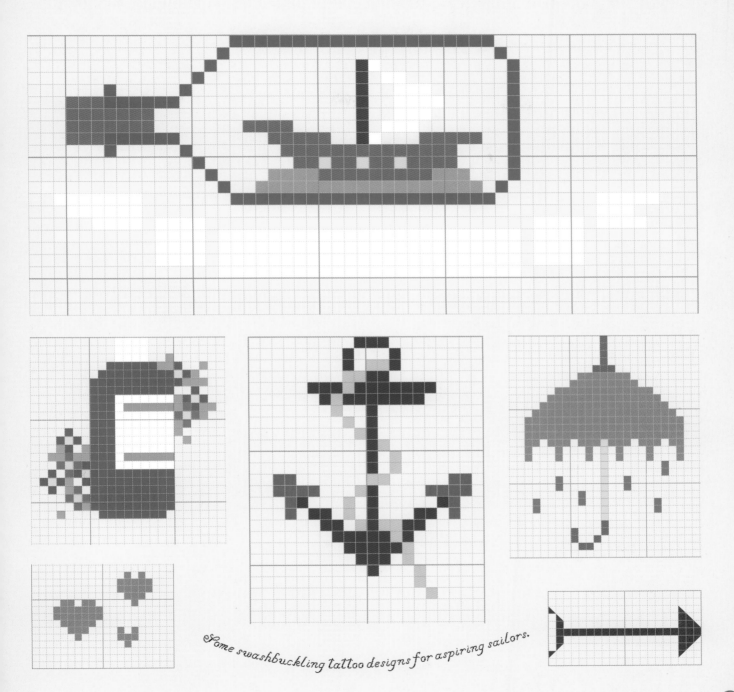

*Some swashbuckling tattoo designs for aspiring sailors.*

# Borders

*These borders can be broken down into smaller motifs.*
*Pick little elements, such as the pizza on its own, to work onto a button.*

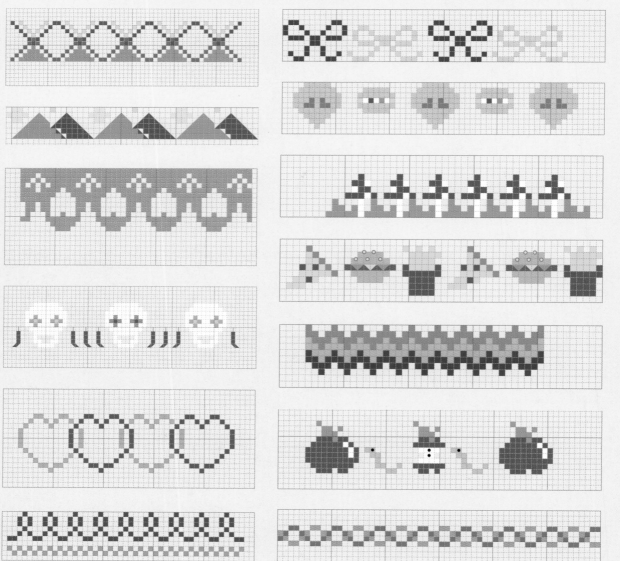

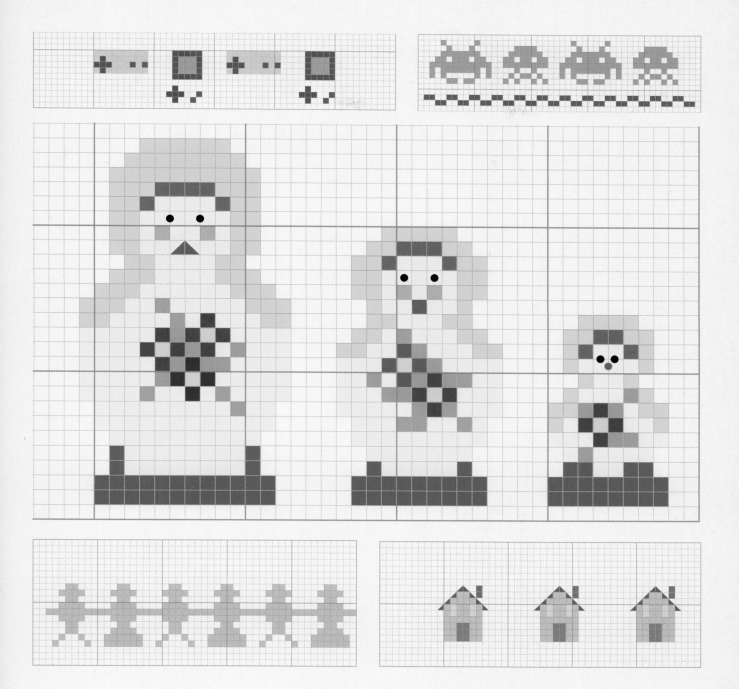

# Home Sweet Home

*These homely motifs are perfect for using in samplers and for house-warming gifts.*

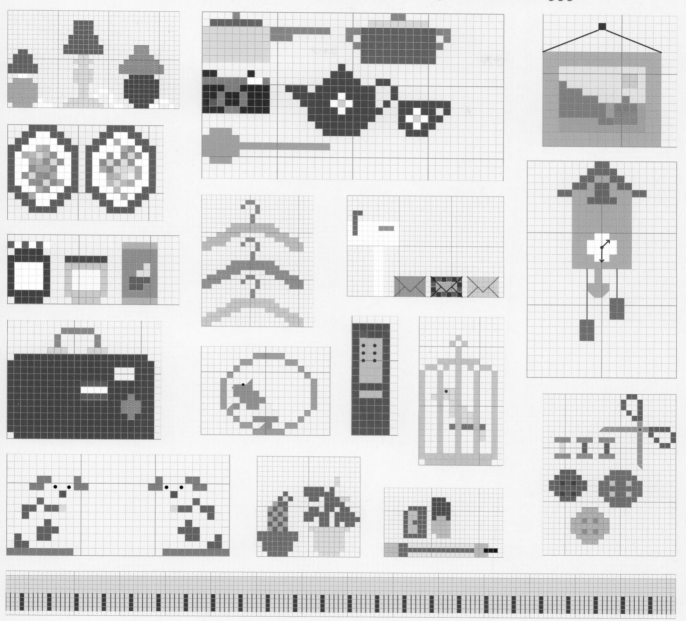

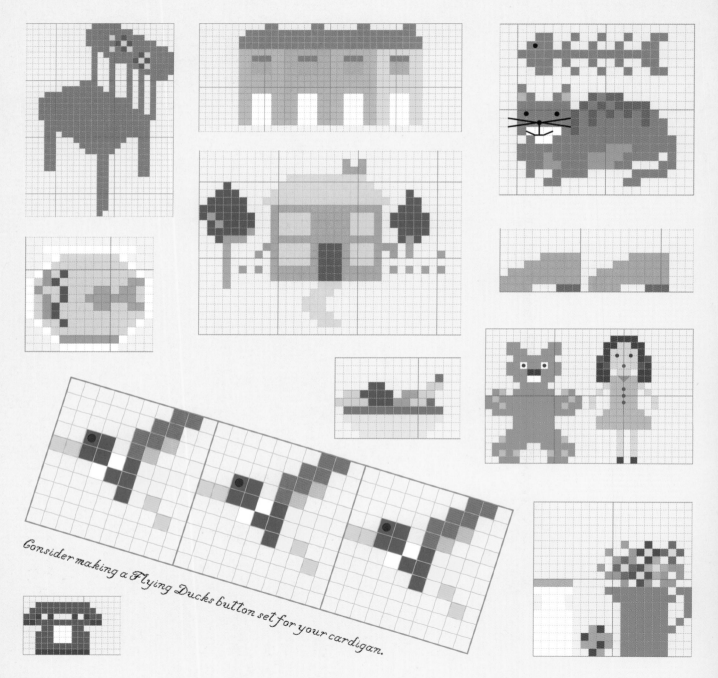

Consider making a Flying Ducks button set for your cardigan.

# Gentlemen

*Take a break from the norm and stop sewing girly things all the time!*

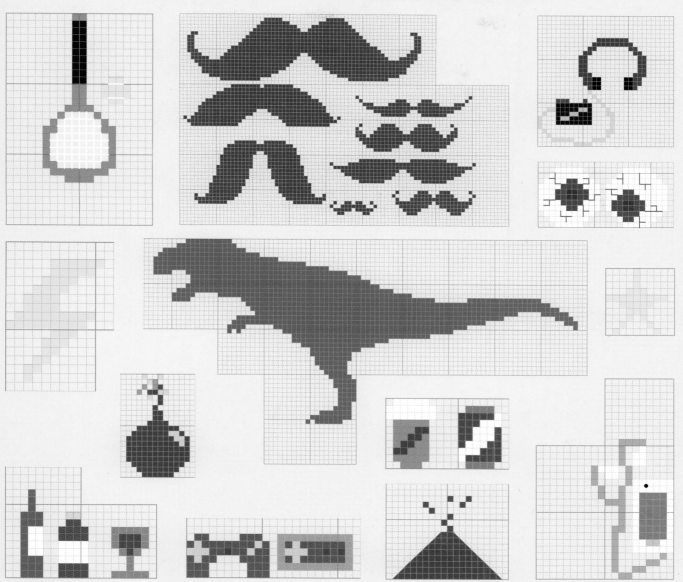

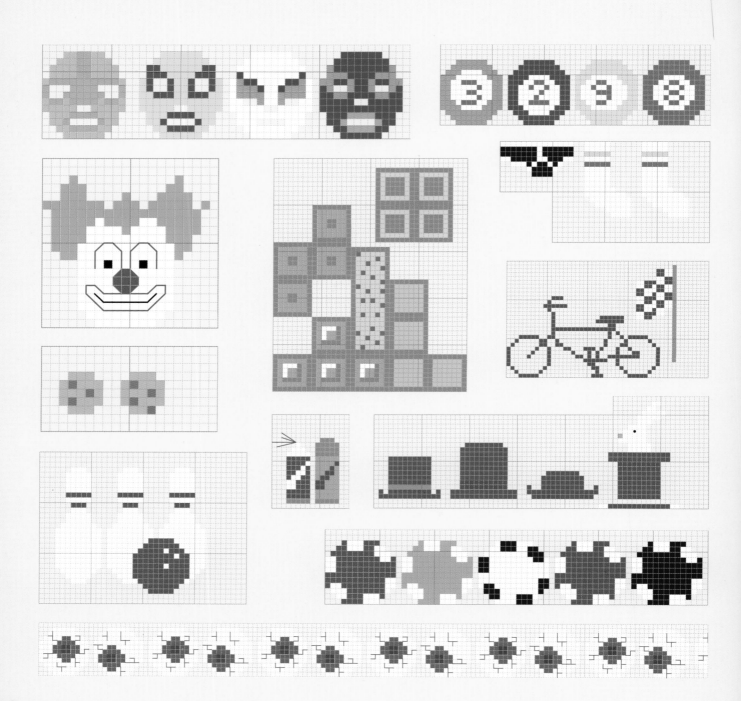

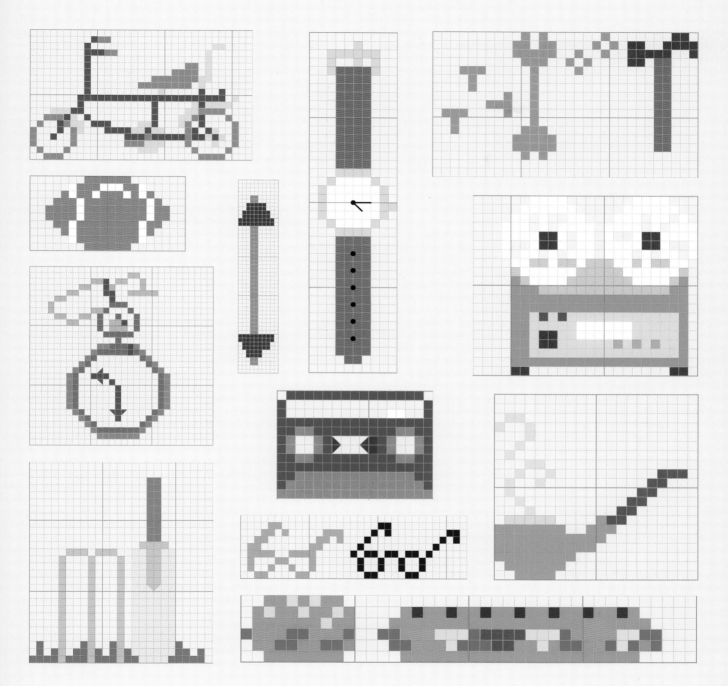

# Alphabet and Numbers

*ABC is easy as 123... Be inventive – what could you spell out on your sampler?*

ABCDEFGHIJKL
MNOPQRSTUVW
XYZ

ABCDEFG
HIJKLMNOPQRSTUV
WXYZ

1234567890

1234567890

0123456789

ABCDEFGHIJK
LMNOPQRST
UVWXYZ

Aa Bb Cc Dd Ee Ff
Gg Hh Ii Jj Kk Ll
Mm Nn Oo Pp Qq
Rr Ss Tt Uu Vv
Ww Xx Yy Zz

abcdefghijklmnopq
rstuvwxyz

# Nature

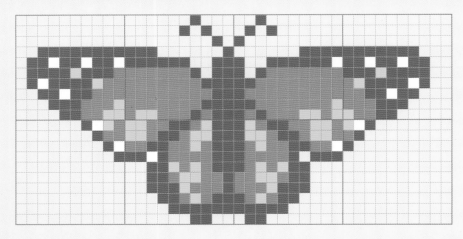

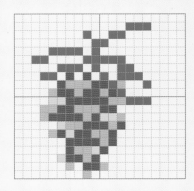

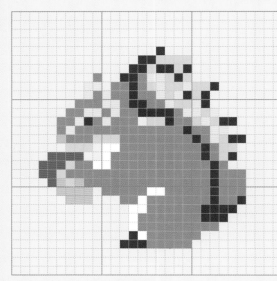

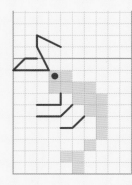

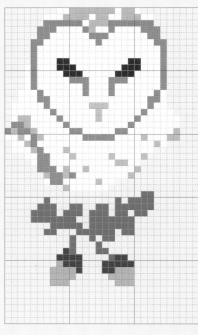

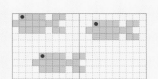

As well as woodland critters, there's a mythical Jackalope – a rabbit with antlers – and a narwhal.

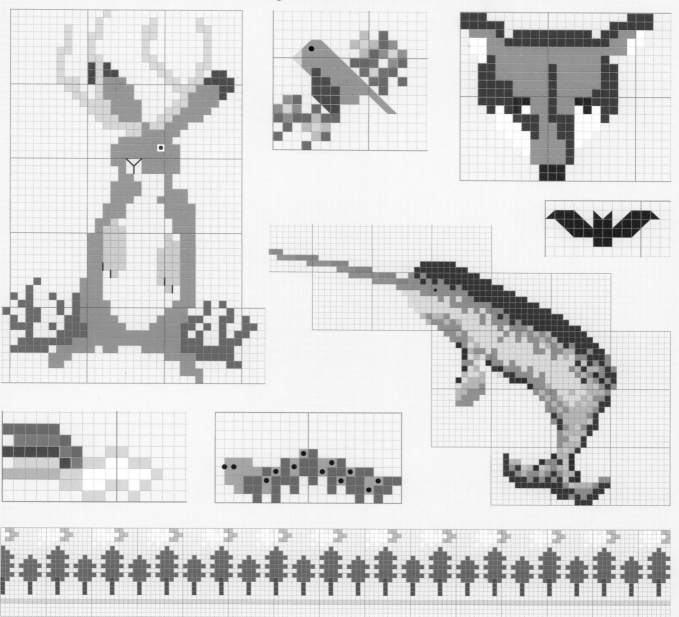

# Valentines and Celebrations

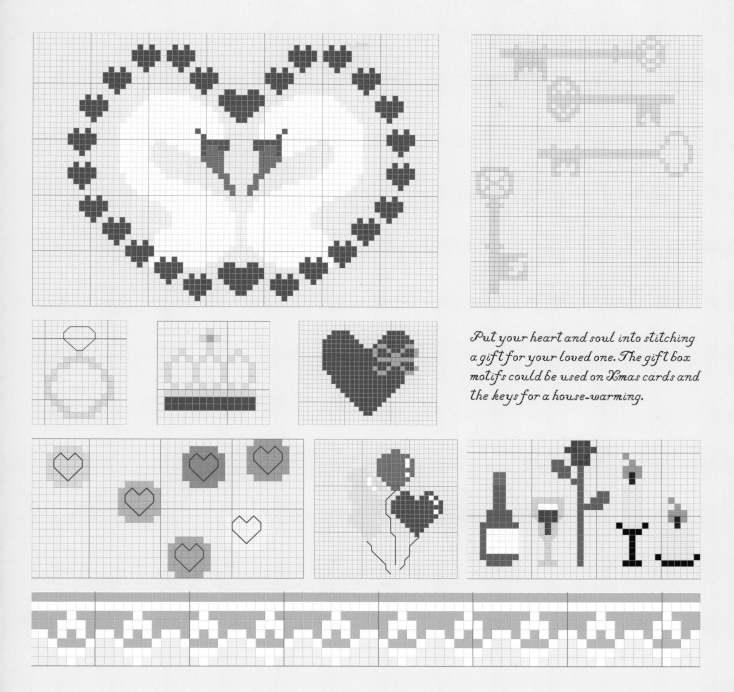

Put your heart and soul into stitching a gift for your loved one. The gift box motifs could be used on Xmas cards and the keys for a house-warming.

# Pop Art

*Use the Lichtenstein-inspired pop art patterns to create
large-scale pieces or use on smaller aida – experiment!*

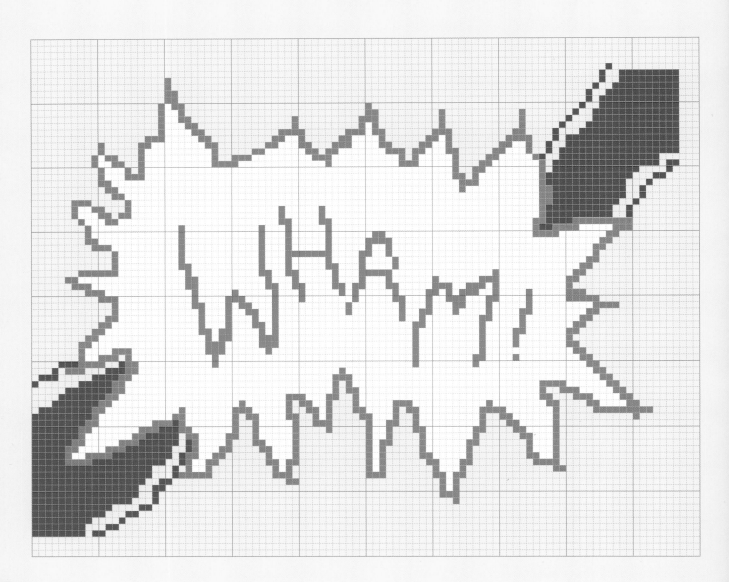

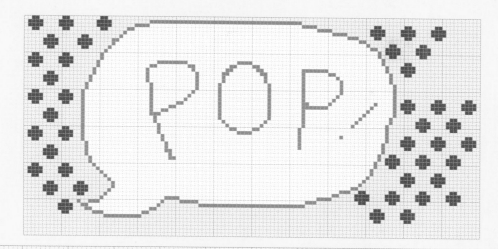

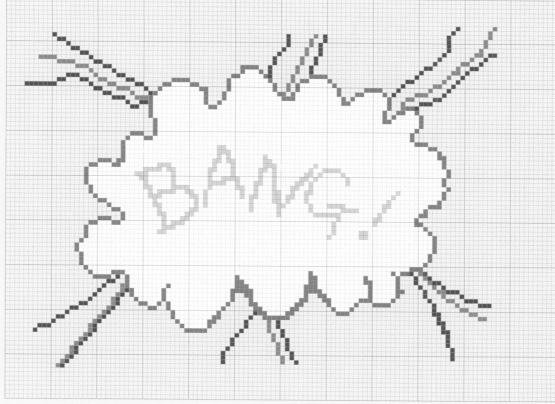

FOR
PEOPLE
WHO KNOW
NEXT TO
NOTHING
ABOUT CROSS
STITCH

VERY EASY
PROJECTS

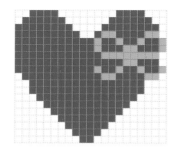

# BUTTONS

XXXXXXXXXXXXXXXXXXXXXXXXXXXXXXXXXXXXXXXXXXXXXXXXXXXXXXXXXXXXXXXXXXXXXXXXXXXXXXXXXXXXXX

I USED TO LOVE VISITING MY GRANDMOTHER AND RUMMAGING THROUGH HER TINS OF OLD BUTTONS. OCCASIONALLY I WOULD FIND A FABRIC BUTTON THAT LOOKED HANDMADE. GRANNY EXPLAINED THAT SHE HAD MADE THEM HERSELF, FROM SCRAPS OF MY GRANDFATHER'S OLD CLOTHES. I LOVED THE IDEA OF BEING ABLE TO MAKE YOUR OWN BUTTONS FROM LITTLE SCRAPS OF FABRIC, AND THIS PROJECT IS A GREAT WAY OF USING UP LEFTOVER PIECES OF AIDA.

Self-cover buttons are inexpensive and available in all sorts of sizes. They can be bought in metal or plastic from your local haberdashery and can be used to make a variety of different things.

As with most of the projects in this book, I have left it to you to decide what design you would like to stitch on your buttons. But do bear in mind that it needs to be small enough to fit on the button you're making. If you browse through the patterns on pages 32–3, you will be able to pick out some of the smaller motifs from the border designs. Alternatively, if you're feeling confident, then create your own design using the graph paper provided on pages 145–9.

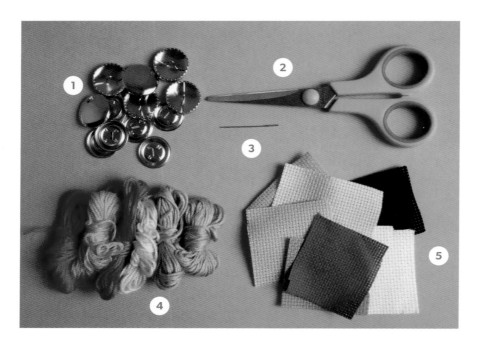

# you will need

1 Metal self-cover buttons

2 Scissors

3 Needle

4 Embroidery thread

5 Aida

## Tips

I prefer to use metal self-cover buttons, as I find them a little stronger than plastic and ideal for thicker fabrics such as aida.

It is possible to purchase a self-cover button tool, which helps you connect all the pieces together without your fingers getting sore.

1 Stitch your chosen mini motif (see pages 32–3 for suggestions) to the centre of your scrap of aida.

2 Place the front of the button face down on the reverse of your stitching (2a). Hold it between your thumb and forefinger and cut around the button approximately ½in (1.25cm) from the edge (2b); you will need this extra aida to fold over the edge.

3 Fold the aida over the edge of the button, pressing it firmly into the teeth. You may wish to use the end of your scissors to push it in really tightly.

4 Click the back of the button into place (4a). Your button is now complete (4b). Repeat the previous steps and make as many buttons in as many different designs as you like.

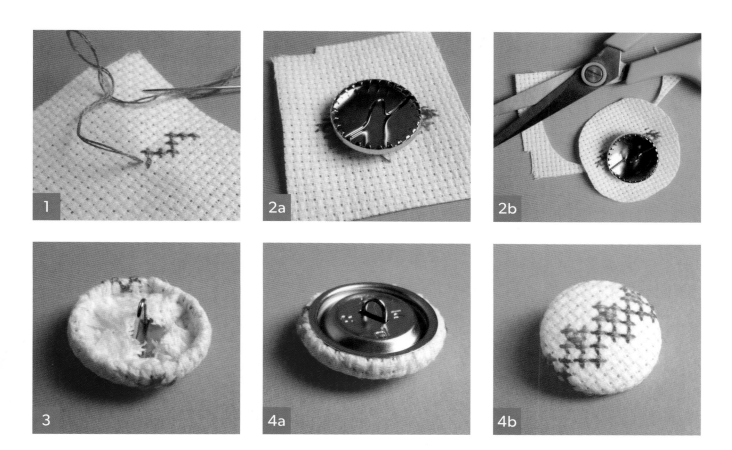

YOU CAN STITCH YOUR BUTTONS ONTO ANYTHING YOU WISH.
WHY NOT UPDATE AN OLD CARDIGAN BY SNIPPING OFF ITS
BUTTONS AND REPLACING THEM WITH YOURS? (JUST MAKE
SURE THAT YOUR BUTTONS FIT THROUGH THE BUTTONHOLES
FIRST!) ALTERNATIVELY, YOU CAN USE THEM PURELY FOR
DECORATION – STITCH THEM ONTO A BAG OR CUSHION,
FOR INSTANCE. THE OPTIONS ARE ENDLESS.

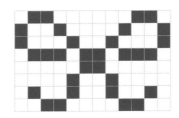

# HAIR BOBBLES

XXXXXXXXXXXXXXXXXXXXXXXXXXXXXXXXXXXXXXXXXXXXXXXXXXXXXXXXXXXXXXXXXXXXXXXXXXXXXXXXXXXX

IF YOU HAVE MASTERED THE ART OF MAKING YOUR OWN CROSS-STITCH BUTTON (SEE PAGES 50–3), YOU ARE GOING TO FIND MAKING A HAIR BOBBLE AS EASY AS PIE! ALL THE MATERIALS REQUIRED ARE THE SAME – WITH THE ADDITION OF SOME THIN, COLOURFUL HAIR ELASTICS – AND THE TECHNIQUE IS THE SAME, TOO.

These hair bobbles are great, cheap, quick gifts to add to party bags for a child's birthday party or as stocking fillers at Christmas. If you are giving them as gifts, wrap them around a pretty piece of card or a vintage playing card to act as quirky packaging.

There are many things you can do with buttons, so get your thinking cap on and experiment. For example, you could thread a button through your shoe laces for instant quirky pumps, or thread a piece of ribbon or decorative cord through the back of the button and tie it around the neck of a bottle of wine as a gift for a friend. Or why not plait some embroidery thread, add a button, and make a friendship bracelet?

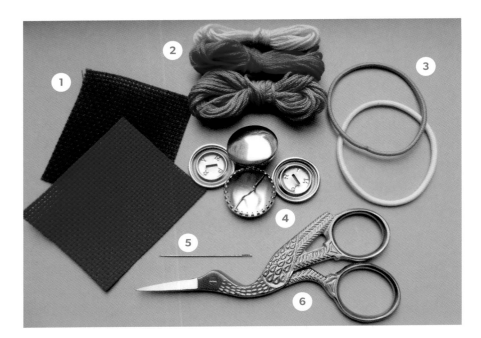

## you will need

1 Aida

2 Embroidery thread

3 Thin hair elastics

4 Self-cover buttons

5 Needle

6 Scissors

Tip Choose a reasonably large button, as anything too small will not show up well in your hair. A good size is ⅞in (2.2cm) or larger.

1 Stitch and assemble your button, following Steps 1–4 of the project on page 52. You will need one button and one hair elastic per bobble.

2 Push the hair elastic a short way through the shank of the button.

3 Loop one end through the other...

4 ... and pull taut to secure it in place. Hey presto – one complete hair bobble. I told you it was easy!

1

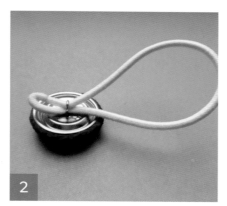

2

3

4

Tip Experiment with different colours – try clashing the colour of the elastic with the colour of your canvas or cross-stitch design.

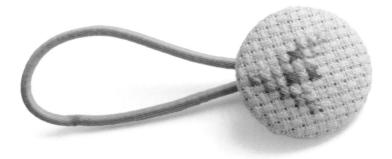

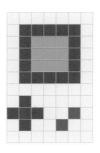

# TIE CLIP

CUFFLINKS ARE THE OBVIOUS CHOICE WHEN IT COMES TO A GIFT FOR EVENTS SUCH AS FATHER'S DAY – BUT WHY NOT SAVE YOUR DAD FROM ARRIVING AT WORK LOOKING BEDRAGGLED ON A WINDY DAY, AND MAKE HIM A TIE CLIP TO HOLD HIS TIE NEATLY IN PLACE? MY DESIGN FEATURES A RETRO HANDHELD VIDEO GAME, BUT YOU COULD CHOOSE WHATEVER HE LIKES MOST – A GOLF CLUB, FOOTBALL OR PERHAPS AN ICE-COOL GLASS OF BEER?

These also look super cute clipped to your shirt pocket, just like a brooch. Wear one while sitting on the train reading your favourite book, then clip it to your page to act as a bookmark.

Tie clips can be bought very cheaply from sites such as eBay, but if you cannot find one, get inventive – a really plain hair clip would work just as well. Make sure it has a nice flat surface (not too thin) that would be suitable for gluing your button to.

## you will need

1 Two-part epoxy adhesive or other strong glue

2 Tie clip

3 Needle

4 Metal self-cover button (⅞in/2.2cm is a good size)

5 Scissors

6 Aida

7 Embroidery thread

Optional: sandpaper
(see Tip on facing page)

Tip Use a really strong glue. Superglue is not appropriate for this type of project, as it is very thin and brittle. You need to look for a glue such as a two-part epoxy resin, which is thick and does not set too quickly, so you have plenty of time to make sure that the piece is positioned correctly before it sets.

1 Stitch your chosen design onto your piece of aida and have your metal self-cover button and scissors at the ready.

2 Using the end of your scissors, prise out the metal loop from inside the front of the self-cover button. This is the button 'shank', which will not be needed in this project. Be careful! You don't want this to ping into your eye or anyone else's.

3 As with the button project (see Step 2, page 52), trim around your stitched design, cutting it about ½in (1.25cm) larger than the front of the button. Fold the edges of the aida over, push the canvas into the teeth and click the back of the button in place. You should now have a button with a nice, smooth back.

1

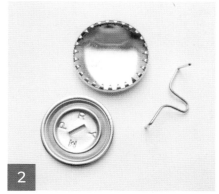

2

3

4a

4b

Tip If you are using a tie clip that is very smooth, roughen the area where you are going to stick the button with a little sandpaper; this will give a better grip and adhesion.

4 Attach the button to the tie clip, following the adhesive manufacturer's instructions. I used a two-part epoxy adhesive, which requires me to mix a tiny amount of each part together, leave for a few seconds, and then apply it to the back of the button (4a). Place the tie clip on top and carefully position it correctly before leaving to dry (4b). You may find that you need to prop it in place so that it doesn't move or slip as it dries.

THE PROCESS USED HERE TO MAKE THE TIE CLIP CAN BE APPLIED TO ANY NUMBER OF PRODUCTS. WHY NOT ATTACH YOUR CROSS-STITCH BUTTON TO A RING, OR MAKE TWO BUTTONS AND ATTACH THEM TO A SET OF CUFFLINKS OR EARRING FINDINGS?

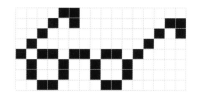

# BADGE

XXXXXXXXXXXXXXXXXXXXXXXXXXXXXXXXXXXXXXXXXXXXXXXXXXXXXXXXXXXXXXXXXXXXXXXXXX

THIS IS ANOTHER VERY SIMPLE PROJECT THAT TEACHES YOU HOW TO MAKE A FELT BADGE THAT YOU CAN ADAPT IN MANY OTHER WAYS. HAVE FUN EXPERIMENTING BY MAKING BADGES IN DIFFERENT SHAPES AND SIZES. WHY NOT MAKE A WHOLE SET USING COMPLEMENTARY DESIGNS? IF YOU CHOOSE THE SMALLER MOTIFS FROM THE PATTERNS ON PAGES 32–3, YOU CAN MAKE YOURSELF A SET OF BADGES IN NO TIME AT ALL.

Why not add a frill of lace around the edge to make it into a fancy brooch? Take a strip of lace, pin it between the aida and the felt and use a simple tiny running stitch (see page 18) to sew it all together.

Alternatively, make a medal. Stitch your badge to the bottom of a short length of ribbon and your brooch pin to the top of the ribbon on the reverse side.

## you will need

1. Felt
2. Circular bottle top or lid to use as a template
3. Aida
4. Needle
5. Scissors
6. Brooch pin
7. Embroidery thread
8. Pencil

1 Stitch a small motif onto your aida (see charts on pages 32–3 for suggestions). Choose a bottle top or lid the size you would like your badge to be, place it over your stitching and press down gently. Remove the lid: it will have left a circular impression around your design. If the design isn't central, repeat the process until you are happy.

2 Place the lid back over the impression and draw around it in pencil. Now cut around the pencil marks to leave a little disc of aida with the design in the centre. This will be the front of your badge.

3 To make the back of the badge, place the lid on a colourful piece of felt and draw around it. Cut out this disc and place it beneath your cut-out piece of aida.

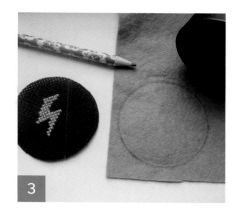

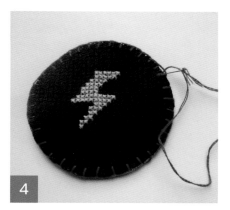

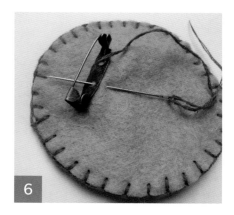

4 Using blanket stitch (see page 18), work your way around the edge of the badge, taking the needle between the layers after the last stitch. The blanket stitching will give the badge a nice edging and should prevent the aida from fraying.

5 Bring the needle out on the back of the badge, either at the centre of the felt backing or towards the top – this will be the position for the brooch pin.

6 Your brooch pin will probably have some small holes running along it. Slip your needle through one of these and make a series of little stitches back and forth between the brooch pin and the felt,

making sure that your needle only slides through the felt. Repeat this process until you have stitched all of the holes in the brooch pin to the felt backing. When you have made your last stitch, slide the end of the thread under your felt and brooch pin and pull the needle back up – ideally at the side of your brooch – and snip off the remaining thread as closely as possible, so that it will never be seen.

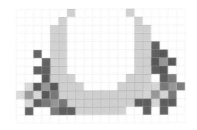

# PATCHES

TRADITIONALLY, FABRIC PATCHES WERE HAND SEWN AND MOST COMMONLY ASSOCIATED WITH THE MILITARY, SPORTS TEAMS OR CLUBS SUCH AS THE GIRL SCOUTS. BUT HERE, WE ARE GOING TO MAKE A PATCH WITH A MODERN TWIST.

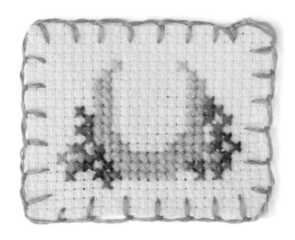

Making a patch is very similar to creating a badge (see pages 62–5). But of course, with a badge you have the freedom of moving it around or taking it off your clothing altogether, while a patch is something a little more permanent. I have demonstrated how to make two very basic square patches, but, as always, there are many other possibilities to explore. Why not cut your patches into unusual shapes? Collect some cookie cutters in shapes such as hearts or flowers, and use them as templates. Place the cookie cutter over your stitched motif, draw around it in pencil and cut out your patch. Easy!

## you will need

1. Embroidery thread
2. Fusible bonding web
3. Aida
4. Needle
5. Scissors

Optional: greaseproof paper

**Tip** If the bonding web did not come with a protective layer, put a piece of greaseproof paper underneath it before you press the layers – otherwise you will end up ironing the patch to your ironing board!

1 Stitch your chosen design (see charts on pages 26–47 for suggestions) onto the aida, then cut the aida to your chosen shape. I opted for a square, so I simply followed the lines in the evenweave fabric to trim it down to the size I wanted. Place the cut-out motif on a piece of fusible bonding web and cut the bonding web to the same size. You should now have a little sandwich of aida at the top, bonding web in the middle, and its protective paper layer at the bottom.

2 Carefully place the layers on an ironing board and press so that the bonding web glues itself to the back of the aida. Let it cool slightly, then peel off the protective layer of paper. You will now be able to see a thin layer of the bonding web on the reverse side of your stitched piece of aida. Don't worry about being able to see your messy stitches: once you have attached the patch to your clothing it won't be seen.

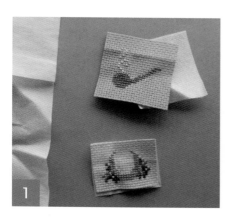
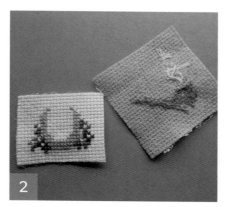
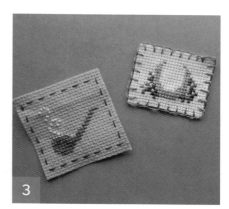

3 You can now choose to finish off your patch however you please. I worked small running stitches around the edge of one and a decorative blanket stitch around the other. Your patches are now ready to be ironed onto your chosen item of clothing.

YOU COULD REALLY GO TO TOWN AND MAKE A LARGE PATCH TO COVER THE BACK OF A DENIM JACKET – BIKER STYLE! SIMPLY USE TRACING PAPER TO TRACE THE BACK PANEL OF YOUR CLOTHING, AND CUT SOME AIDA TO SIZE. WORK YOUR DESIGN, THEN IRON IT ONTO THE ITEM OF CLOTHING. YOU MAY WISH TO FURTHER STITCH AROUND THE EDGES TO REALLY FINISH IT OFF.

# GREETINGS CARD

MAKING YOUR OWN GREETINGS CARD IS SO SIMPLE, AND THE BEST THING ABOUT THESE CARDS IS THAT THEY ARE LIKE LITTLE WORKS OF ART: JUST POP THEM IN A PICTURE FRAME TO MOUNT ON THE WALL AND THEY BECOME AN INSTANT KEEPSAKE. THE CARD AND THE ENVELOPE DON'T HAVE TO BE THE SAME COLOUR. INSTEAD, EXPERIMENT WITH COMPLEMENTARY – OR EVEN CLASHING – COLOURS.

Use a ready-made aperture card for this: they have a pre-cut frame for your design, with another flap of card that you fold over to cover the messy reverse of your stitching. Aperture cards come in many different colours and sizes, and some even have novelty heart-shaped windows. You can also get aperture bookmarks, so you could make a gift for your favourite bookworm.

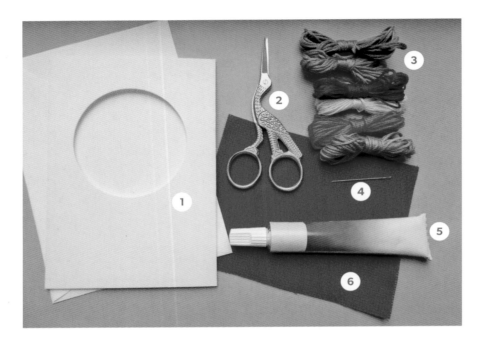

## you will need

1. Aperture card with envelope
2. Scissors
3. Embroidery thread
4. Needle
5. All-purpose glue
6. Aida

Tip Before you do anything, make sure that the area you are working on is as clean as possible, as you want to avoid getting any crumbs or smudges on your card.

1 Choose the design you want for your card. What's the occasion? Who's it for? What colours do they like? I chose the bicycle design from page 38 and used 14-count aida. Stitch your design in place.

2 Open the card and position the 'window' over your design, making sure it is centred. Cut the aida to approximately 1in (2.5cm) bigger all around than the window.

3 Open the card and squeeze some little dots of glue around the edge of the 'window' and the top and bottom edges of the card – but not too close to the edge, as you do not want the glue to ooze out when you close the card.

1

2

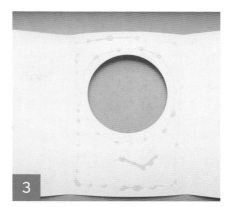

3

4

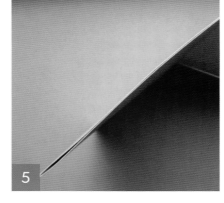

5

4 Place the piece of aida face down over the window and, while holding it in place, turn the card over to check its position from the front. When you are happy with the placement, smooth the fabric down and press down the left-hand side of your card.

5 You will need to check for any gaps where you have glued your card together. Add a tiny drop of glue using either a brush or a cocktail stick if it is easier, to avoid making a mess. Once all the edges are sealed neatly, your work is done. Leave the card to dry somewhere clean, away from grubby fingertips.

Tip If the aida looks a little creased when you have finished your stitching, you may need to give it a gentle press with an iron before you apply it to the card. Use a low heat setting and protect your work by putting a piece of waste fabric over the top (again, make sure it is clean, as it will be making contact with your work). Press the piece gently face down until the creases have disappeared.

# NEEDLE CASE

I HAVE BEEN KNOWN TO LEAVE PINS AND NEEDLES LYING AROUND, AND THEY USUALLY END UP IN SOMEONE'S FOOT! I LOVE QUIRKY PINCUSHIONS, BUT NEEDLE CASES ARE SO PRETTY AND ARE ALSO REALLY EASY TO MAKE.

A needle case is like a fabric book, with a single page to keep your pins or needles safe in. There are no set rules for what size or shape a needle case should be. I opted for roughly 3½ x 4in (9 x 10cm) to make it pocket-sized and small enough to carry around in my bag for sewing on the go.

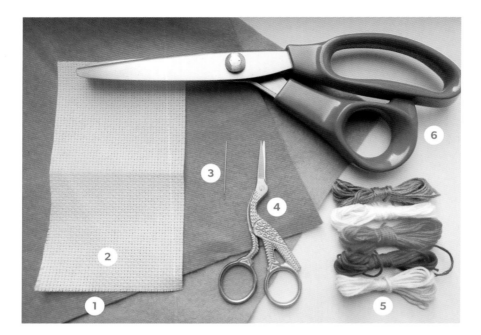

## you will need

1. Felt in two colours: one piece approx. 7½ x 3½in (19 x 9cm), the other approx. 5 x 2¼in (13 x 6cm)

2. Aida, approx. 2¾ x 2¼in (7 x 6cm)

3. Needle

4. Scissors

5. Embroidery thread

6. Pinking shears

1 Work your chosen design (see charts on pages 26–47 for suggestions) onto the aida. Using pinking shears, snip around the edges of each piece of felt. (This is purely for decorative effect.)

2 The larger piece of felt will be the cover of the needle case. Fold it in half like a book, and attach your completed cross-stitch design to the centre of the front with a simple running stitch (see page 18), using the holes in the aida as a guide to keep your stitches straight and even.

3 Open the cover up. Fold the smaller piece of felt in half and place it in the middle of the cover, aligning the fold with the fold in the cover. This will become the inside page of the needle case.

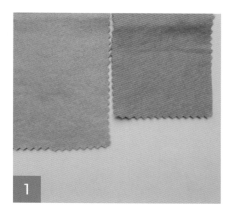

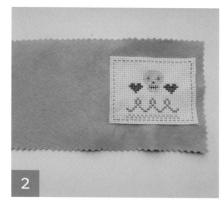

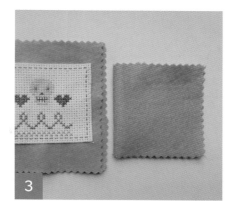

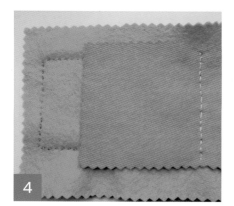

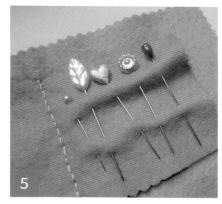

Tips Consider adding an extra 'page' of felt into your needle case so that you can store more pins and needles. You could make each page a different colour – but do not add too many or your case will get quite bulky.

Make sure the inner pages are hidden from view when the case is closed by always making your cover page a little bigger in size.

4 With a contrasting colour of thread, attach the inside page to the cover using back stitch or running stitch (see page 18). Don't worry about the appearance of the stitches too much – just do them as neatly as you can.

5 Gather your pins and needles and stick them into the inside page of the needle case. You will never lose a pin again!

EASY
PROJECTS

FOR PEOPLE
WHO KNOW
ENOUGH
TO KNOW THAT
THEY DO NOT KNOW
EVERYTHING

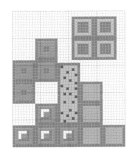

# GADGET CASE

I REALLY LIKE BLACK AIDA. WELL, I LIKE ALL COLOURS THAT ARE A BREAK FROM THE BORING CREAM – BUT I PARTICULARLY LIKE WORKING ON BLACK, AS IT CAN MAKE THE COLOURS OF YOUR FLOSS 'POP'! IT IS ALSO GREAT FOR RETRO COMPUTER GAME DESIGNS AND NEVER LOOKS TOO OLD-FASHIONED OR GIRLY. THE TROUBLE IS, SINCE IT IS SO DARK, IT CAN BE ALMOST IMPOSSIBLE TO SEE THE HOLES IN THE FABRIC, WHICH CAN MAKE STITCHING TRICKY. THIS PROJECT IS A GOOD INTRODUCTION – AND OVERLEAF YOU'LL FIND A FEW TIPS TO MAKE THE PROCESS A LITTLE EASIER.

When choosing the design for your gadget case, decide whether you want one that is small enough to sit at the front of the case or one that will cover most of the aida. I chose the retro computer game design from page 38, as it is the perfect size to sit at the front of my case and also suits the black aida. It's a good idea to draw around your gadget on a sheet of graph paper, so that you have an idea of how much space you have to work with, and doodle a design in this space. You will see that I have not given specific measurements for the aida, as the amount will depend on the size of the gadget. But as a general guide you will need a piece that can wrap around the gadget about three times its width, with a little spare, and is tall enough to cover the gadget completely.

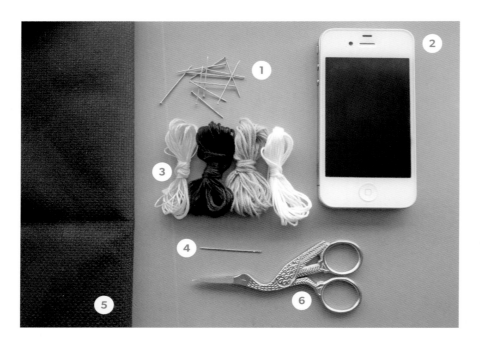

## you will need

1. Pins
2. Gadget of your choice
3. Embroidery thread
4. Needle
5. Aida
6. Scissors

Tip When working with black aida, make sure you work in bright natural light or use a daylight bulb in your lamp, and place a piece of white paper or fabric on your lap behind the aida to make it easier to see where the holes are.

1 Following the tips on the left for working with black aida, work your chosen design. Place your gadget on the aida, positioning the design where you would like it to sit (I placed mine at the front of my gadget), and fold the fabric around. You want to create a nice cushioned 'blanket' to wrap your gadget in, so you may even want enough aida to have two layers around your gadget.

2 Allow enough aida to fold around the case with a generous overlap, and also plenty at the top and bottom, to fold inside. Make some firm creases as guidelines for where the fabric will fold around the gadget. Cut away any excess aida, using the lines in the evenweave as a guide to cut straight edges.

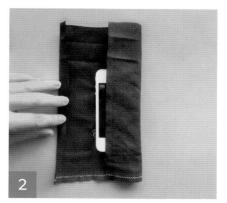

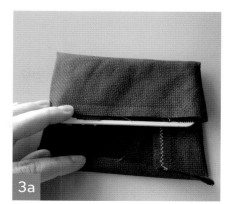

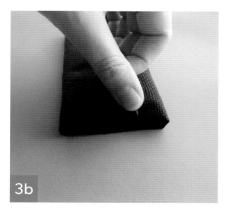

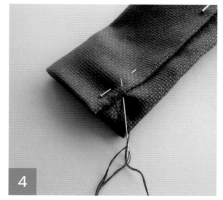

3 Fold in all the edges so that there are no raw edges at the top, bottom, or sides of the case (3a). Keeping your gadget wrapped in its new 'blanket', make sure you are happy with the size and fit of the aida (3b). You do not want to wrap the aida so tightly that you cannot remove your gadget easily.

4 Pin the aida in place along the length of the gadget case. Check again that you can slide the gadget in and out easily. Using black embroidery thread or cotton, stitch the seam, using small running stitches (see page 18) or any small straight stitches you are comfortable with; do not worry too much about what the stitches look like, as they will be barely visible. Lose the end of the thread under the hem and snip off. Remove the pins.

5 Once again, slip the gadget into the aida and pinch together the two layers of aida at the bottom. This will form the base of the case. Stitch along here, just as you did up the side. (You may find it easier to not bother pinning this part, as it is so small. I even kept my gadget inside as I stitched, to help me gauge where it would sit.) Hey presto – you now have one complete gadget case!

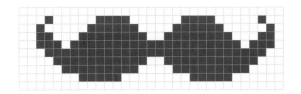

# COASTERS

THERE ARE A LOT OF QUIRKY ITEMS ON THE MARKET THAT ENABLE YOU TO FINISH OFF YOUR CROSS-STITCH PROJECTS NICELY. AS WELL AS PICTURE FRAMES, YOU CAN ALSO FIND PLASTIC DRINKS COASTERS, KEY RINGS AND ITEMS SUCH AS PAPERWEIGHTS TO HELP YOU TRANSFORM YOUR HUMBLE MOTIF INTO A READY-MADE GIFT.

In this project I am going to explain just how simple it is to make a couple of drinks coasters. You could easily create a larger set to keep for yourself or as a housewarming gift for a friend packaged in a nice box.

You will need to purchase coasters that are specifically made for craft projects. They will be clear and have a removable back, allowing you to place your stitching inside. I was fortunate enough to find mine in my local craft store, but eBay is a good place to search for them.

## you will need

1. Aida
2. Plastic drinks coasters
3. Scissors
4. Needle
5. Pencil
6. Embroidery thread

Optional: thin cotton fabric for reverse of coaster

Tip Instead of using plain fabric for the reverse side of your coaster, you could stitch an identical design on another piece of aida so that it doesn't matter which way up the coaster is placed. Alternatively, why not stitch a different design so you can ring the changes? Just make sure you can fit the two pieces of aida in your coasters when they're shut.

1 Draw around your coaster in pencil on graph paper (see pages 145–9). This will allow you to gauge what size the design needs to be.

2 Work your chosen design (see charts on pages 26–47 for suggestions) onto the aida. Once complete, place one of the coasters on top, positioning the design in the centre. Draw around the edge in pencil.

3 Cut out the design (3a) and place the stitching inside the coaster (3b). You may need to trim the edges down to allow it to sit snugly – trim off a tiny piece at a time. If you like, you can cut a piece of thin cotton fabric the same size as your finished work and insert it in the coaster so that it covers the stitches on the back of the piece. Click the back of the coaster in place and you're finished.

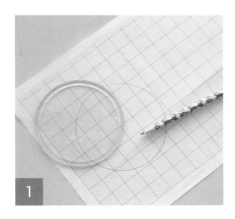

1

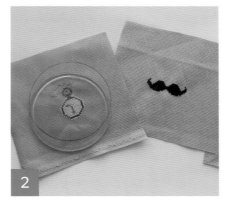

2

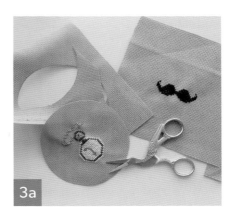

3a

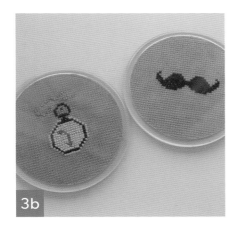

3b

CONSIDER MAKING A FULL SET OF THEMED DESIGNS
AS A GIFT, OR FOR YOUR OWN HOME. JUST ADD A MUG
OF HOT TEA OR A COOL BEER!

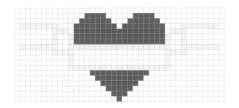

# MINI SAMPLERS

XXXXXXXXXXXXXXXXXXXXXXXXXXXXXXXXXXXXXXXXXXXXXXXXXXXXXXXXXXXXXXXXXXXXXXXXXXXXXXXXXX

EMBROIDERY HOOPS ARE USUALLY USED TO HELP KEEP YOUR AIDA TAUT WHILE WORKING ON IT, BUT THEY CAN ALSO DOUBLE AS READY-MADE FRAMES FOR YOUR WORK, WITH THE LOOP AT THE TOP ACTING AS THE PERFECT DEVICE TO HOOK ONTO A NAIL ON YOUR WALL. THESE MINI HOOPS ALLOW YOU TO WHIP UP LITTLE PICTURES IN NO TIME AT ALL!

Why not make a set of different-sized samplers, each with a different design, to hang as a collection of themed pictures on your wall? Alternatively, you could stitch a letter onto each hoop so that they spell out a word or message of your choice.

If you prefer, you can add a loop of fancy ribbon or braid to the metal screw at the top of your hoop so that your work can easily be hung, or use this place to tie a decorative bow.

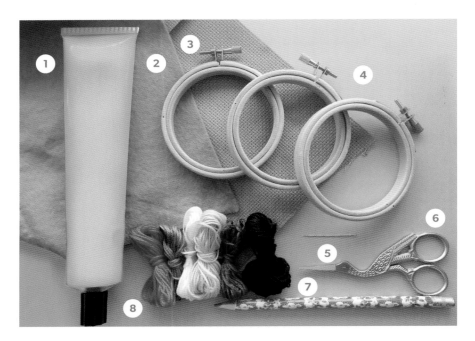

## you will need

1. All-purpose glue
2. Felt
3. Aida
4. Embroidery hoops
5. Needle
6. Scissors
7. Pencil
8. Embroidery thread

Tip It is up to you whether you stitch your design before you add it to the hoop or whether you work it inside the hoop. I find it easier to stitch without using the hoop, as I can manipulate the fabric more easily and work much faster. If you wish to do the same, simply put the fabric in the hoop after you have completed your stitching, as described in Step 1.

1 Unscrew the embroidery hoop to separate it into two rings. Place the aida over the ring that does not have the screw at the top. This hoop remains at the back of your work. Place the other hoop over the top of the aida, pulling the fabric gently so that it is taut; make sure that the aida sits comfortably in the hoop and that the evenweave holes in the fabric are not distorted.

2 When you have set all your stitched motifs into their embroidery hoops, trim off the excess fabric, leaving about 1in (2.5cm) of aida around the edges of your work.

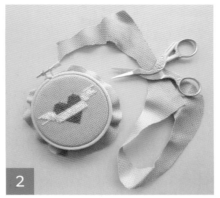

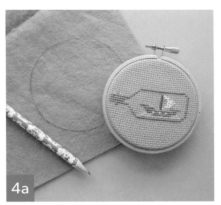

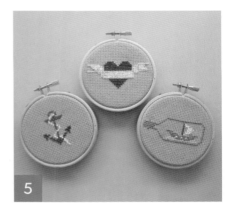

3 Use unwanted embroidery thread or cotton thread to gather all the spare aida at the back of your work. Insert the needle and thread at one side of the hoop, then take it diagonally across to the opposite side, and repeat until all the excess aida has been gathered. You can be as messy as you like here, as this part will not be seen – but it does need to be pulled fairly tight so that it all gets held in place securely.

4 Using a pencil, draw around the hoop on a piece of felt (4a). You can use a pen instead of a pencil, of course, but be careful not to mark your wooden hoop with any ink, as it is impossible to remove. Cut out the disc of felt, apply a little glue all around the edge of the gathered fabric (4b), and place the disc of felt on top. Rub away any excess glue and trim any overhanging felt. Your mini sampler now has a nice clean backing to it.

5 Repeat the instructions to make as many samplers as you like. Group them to make an attractive wall feature, or make them up as gifts for friends.

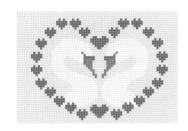

# MINI CUSHION

When I was young, my grandmother had little lavender pillows in her bedroom, as she believed the scent would help her to sleep. Here you will find the basic steps to make your own cross-stitch cushion, which can either be made really small and filled entirely with lavender, or larger and have a small lavender-filled pouch inserted inside it.

If you would like to make a larger cushion but still have the scent of lavender, create a little pouch of lavender to insert inside by stitching two square pieces of cotton fabric together in the same way as the main cushion. Fill the pouch with the lavender and stitch up the gap in the sides. Push the lavender-filled pouch inside your cushion, along with the wadding or toy filling to complete.

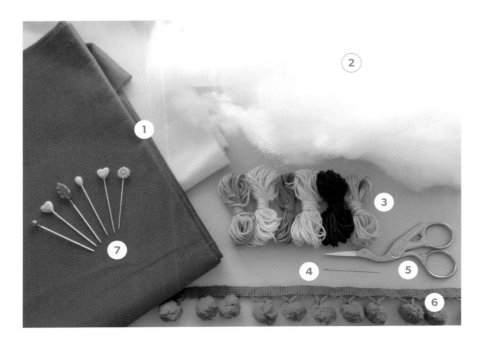

## you will need

1. Aida
2. Wadding or polyester toy filling
3. Embroidery floss or cotton
4. Needle
5. Scissors
6. Ribbon or fancy trim
7. Pins

Optional: dried lavender

1 Decide what size of cushion you want to make. Cut two pieces of aida 1in (2.5cm) bigger all around. Stitch your chosen designs onto the two pieces. You may find it helpful to first sketch some designs to scale on graph paper (see pages 145–9); however, I leapt straight in and stitched the swan motif to one side and a mismatch of motifs on the back. I didn't plan where they would go – I just improvised. It's up to you.

2 With right sides together, pin the two pieces of aida together. Using the evenly spaced holes in the evenweave as your guide, backstitch all around the sides, 1in (2.5cm) from the edge. Leave a gap at the bottom so that you can stuff your cushion.

3 Using your scissors, cut off each corner, taking care not to cut through any of the stitches. This helps you to create sharp, pointy corners.

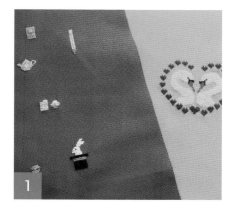

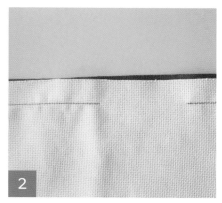

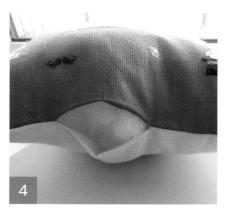

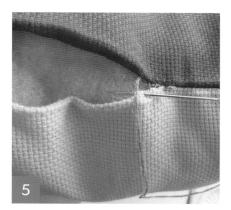

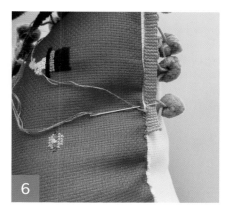

4 Remove the pins and turn the cushion cover inside out through the gap you left in Step 2. Use your hand or the tips of your scissors to push out each corner to a nice point. If you are making a large cushion, push the wadding or toy filling inside the cushion cover, being sure to fill all the corners. Otherwise, fill with lavender.

5 Stitch up the gap using small, straight stitches. You can use any colour of thread that you like, as the stitches will not be visible once you have added the trim, but keep your stitches small and discreet. Lose the end of the thread in the seam and snip it off.

6 Hold one end of the trim against the base of your cushion and work a couple of small stitches to keep it in place. This time, use an embroidery floss or cotton that matches the trim, as the stitches here will be more noticeable. Work your way all around the cushion until you meet the end of the trim. Cut, so that the two ends meet, then stitch the ends together. You now have a cushion with a pretty trim running all around the edge.

# TRADITIONAL SAMPLER

TRADITIONALLY, SAMPLERS WERE MADE AS A CHANCE TO EXPERIMENT WITH DIFFERENT STITCHES. OFTEN THEY INCLUDED PERSONAL DETAILS, SUCH AS THE MAKER'S NAME AND DATE OF BIRTH, AND COMMON MOTIFS MAY HAVE INCLUDED THE ALPHABET. ALTHOUGH THEY WERE USUALLY MADE UP OF DIFFERENT TYPES OF STITCHES, YOU CAN MAKE YOUR OWN VERSION USING CROSS STITCH ALONE.

Think about the motifs you could use to make the sampler personal to you. I started by stitching the house on page 36 and 'Home Sweet Home' message from the chart on page 34 and then added various other motifs around it for an eclectic look.

## you will need

**1** Aida

**2** All-purpose glue

**3** Felt

**4** Pencil

**5** Needle

**6** Scissors

**7** Embroidery hoop

**8** Embroidery thread

Tip If you want to make a sampler that includes text, you will need to sketch your design onto graph paper first (see pages 145–9). Count an even number of squares between each letter of your text, so that your words are evenly spaced.

1 Once you have stitched your design, place it in your embroidery hoop – unless, of course, you have already been working on it in the hoop. Make sure that it is nice and taut and all lines of evenweave are straight and haven't been pulled out of shape. Place the hoop on a sheet of felt and draw around the edge. Cut out the felt; this will be used to cover the back of your work.

2 Trim off the excess aida so that there is only about 1in (2.5cm) more all around – enough to fold over the edge of the hoop. Using any spare unwanted floss or some strong cotton, make a series of diagonal stitches across the hoop to pull in all the edges of aida. Run a line of glue around the edge.

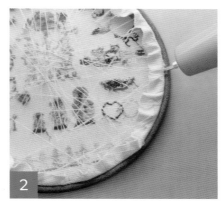

Tip If you are working on a large piece, it may help to mark the centre point by folding your aida and then marking the centre of your design on your graph paper by counting the squares both across the page and down the middle.

3 Place the circle of felt on top and pull it gently so that it fits neatly across the back of your work, wiping off any excess glue as you go (3a). You may need to trim the edges of felt again so that you cannot see any from the front of your work. And there you have it – one traditional-style sampler (3b).

I ADMIT IT, I AM GUILTY OF DIVING STRAIGHT INTO A LARGE PIECE OF AIDA WITHOUT MARKING MY CENTRE POINT (SEE TIP ABOVE). BUT, I USE ANY 'WASTE' AIDA FOR SMALLER PROJECTS SUCH AS THE BUTTONS ON PAGE 50. NOW YOU CAN DO THE SAME – NOTHING EVER NEEDS TO GO TO WASTE!

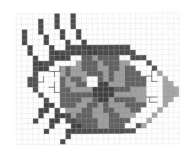

# EYE MASK

THIS FUN AND COLOURFUL EYE MASK IS PERFECT FOR KEEPING OUT THE LIGHT AND HELPING YOU TO GET A RESTFUL NIGHT'S SLEEP. I RECOMMEND USING A BRIGHTLY COLOURED AIDA AND EMBROIDERY THREAD WITH A CONTRASTING RIBBON.

Experiment with different widths of ribbon. A wider ribbon, as pictured, creates a much fuller bow. It is better to go for a very soft, satin ribbon, as it will be more comfortable to sleep in.

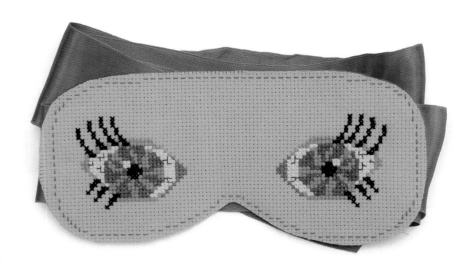

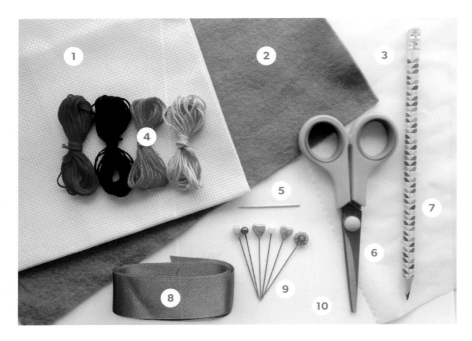

## you will need

1. Aida, 12 x 8in (30 x 20cm)

2. Felt, 8 x 4in (20 x 10cm)

3. Pen or pencil

4. Embroidery thread

5. Needle

6. Scissors

7. Tracing paper

8. 1yd (100cm) ribbon, 1in (2.5cm) wide

9. Pins

10. Paper

Tip For a more luxurious eye mask, cut a thin piece of cotton wadding to the same size as the eye mask and sandwich it in between the front and back pieces. Use a soft, satin fabric as the backing fabric, instead of felt.

1 Following the chart on page 29, stitch the eyes onto the aida. Trace the template on page 104 onto paper and cut out.

2 Place your paper pattern over the stitched eyes, positioning it so that the eyes are fairly central. Pin the pattern in place.

3 Cut around the edge of the pattern. Remove the pins and pattern. You now have the front of the mask. Pin the pattern to the felt and cut around it; this will form the back of the mask.

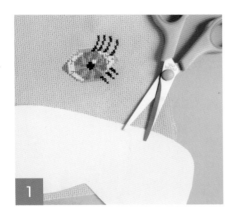

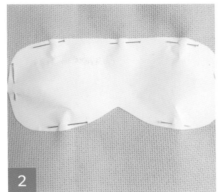

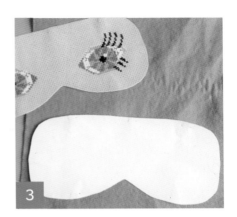

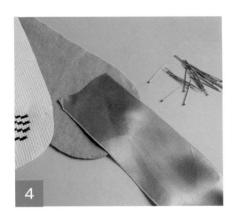

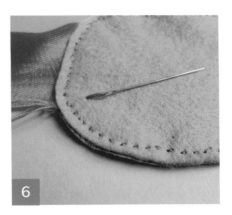

4 Cut the ribbon in half and place one end of each piece on the felt at each side of the mask, with at least 1in (2.5cm) of the ribbon inside the mask to make sure it will be secure. Place the front of the mask on top and pin around the edges to hold the aida, felt and ribbon together.

5 Take a length of embroidery thread and carefully pull away two strands. Thread the needle and work a line of running stitch around the edge of the mask. The evenweave of the aida makes it really easy to do an evenly spaced running stitch that looks neat on the reverse of your mask as well.

6 To avoid having a knot from the end of your thread on show, take the needle between the felt and aida, pull it through the felt, and cut the end of the thread as close to the felt as possible, leaving the end of the thread sandwiched between the layers and out of sight. Your mask is now complete – sweet dreams!

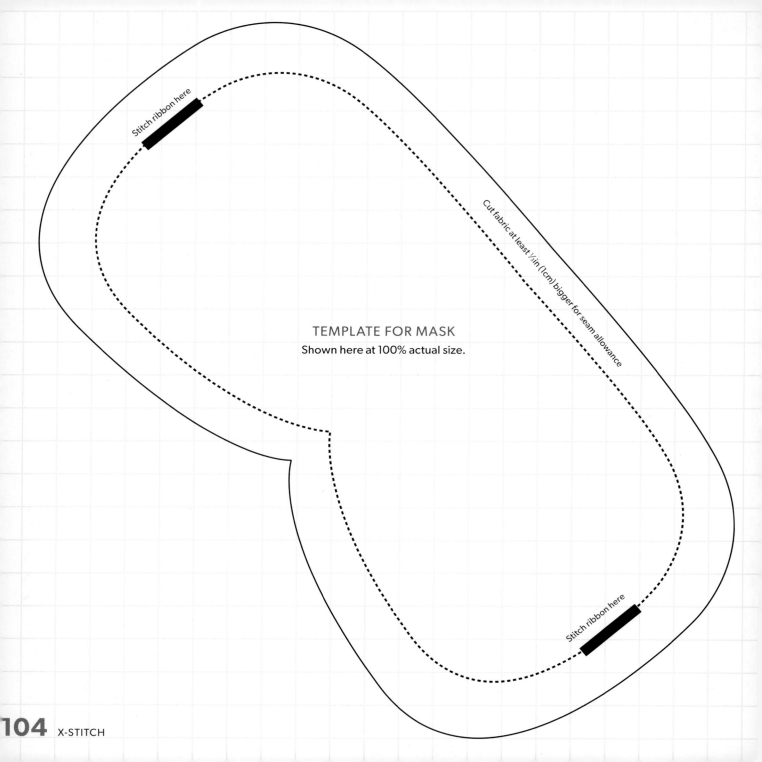

Stitch ribbon here

Cut fabric at least ⅓in (1cm) bigger for seam allowance

TEMPLATE FOR MASK

Shown here at 100% actual size.

Stitch ribbon here

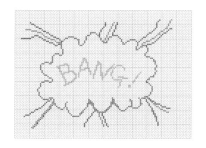

# POP ART CANVASES

BINCA IS A LARGE-SCALE, EVENWEAVE FABRIC THAT CHILDREN USE TO PRACTISE THEIR STITCHING ON, USING KNITTING WOOL AND A LARGE-EYED NEEDLE INSTEAD OF EMBROIDERY THREAD; THE LARGE SCALE MAKES IT MUCH EASIER TO WORK ON. PROJECTS ON BINCA CAN BE TURNED AROUND QUITE QUICKLY. I HAVE DEMONSTRATED HOW TO MAKE A BOLD, POP ART-INSPIRED SET OF THREE CANVASES AND HAVE INCLUDED THE CHARTS FOR THESE ON PAGES 46–7.

Taking the basic principles of working with binca, you could make these canvases into many other things. Instead of attaching to the canvas frame, why not cover the binca in stitches to make it a little more robust, stitch a hem around the edge and use it as a lightweight rug? Alternatively, you could make a large cushion by doubling the amount of fabric required and filling it with wadding, just like the mini cushion on page 92.

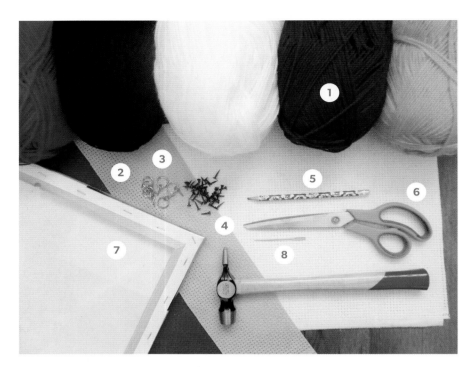

## you will need

1. Wool – can be cheap acrylic

2. Binca

3. Screw-in eyelets

4. Staple gun or small tacks and a hammer

5. Pencil

6. Scissors

7. Three cheap ready-made canvases or wooden frames

8. Large-eyed needle (tapestry needle or a child's plastic needle)

1 First of all, get your frames ready. If you have bought cheap, ready-made canvases, as I did, then tear off all the canvas (1a). Do not worry too much about removing all the staples – only do so if they are loose or look too messy. Once you have done this, put the frames to one side (1b).

2 Work your pop art designs onto binca, using the wool in exactly the same way as you would use embroidery thread when cross stitching on aida – but only use one strand of wool. When your work is complete, place the frame on the back of the stitching and trim off any excess binca, making sure you keep enough to fold over the edges of the frame.

3 Now stretch your work over the frame. It may be easier to use a staple gun, but I had tacks to hand so I used those instead. Bring the canvas over the top edge of the frame in the middle of one side and hammer a pin or tack into the wood to hold the fabric in place. Now pull the binca over the bottom edge of the frame so that it is taut, and fix another pin or tack in place in the middle of this edge.

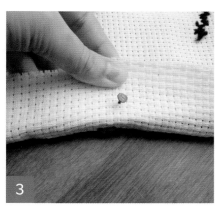

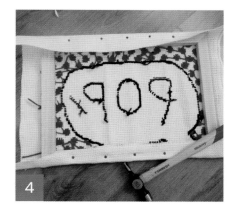

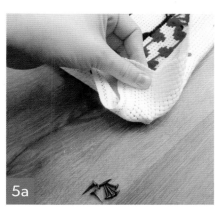

4 Working outwards from either side of the central tack, insert tacks along the top and bottom edges of the frame. Check before you insert each tack that the binca is taut and not wonky. Tack the sides of the frame in the same way.

5 When you get to the corners, pull the corner of the binca inwards over the frame edge (5a) and then fold either side on top of it (5b) and tack it in place. This will give you a neat, mitred corner.

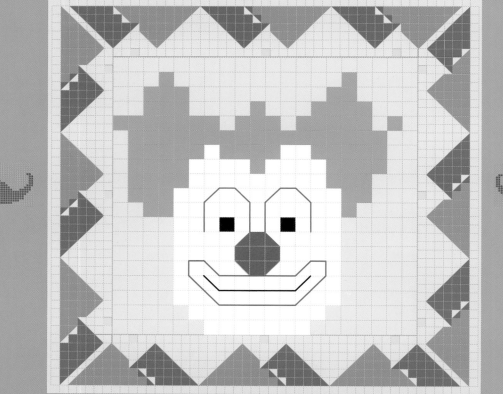

YOU HAD ME IN STITCHES

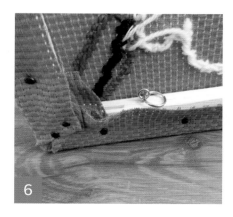

WHILE POP ART TYPICALLY USES PRIMARY COLOURS, AS WITH ALL THE PROJECTS IN THIS BOOK THERE IS FREEDOM TO EXPERIMENT WITH COLOUR. YOU CAN ALSO BUY CIRCULAR CANVASES, WHICH MAY BE A FUN ALTERNATIVE.

6 Once all the canvas has been tacked in place, you will need to add some eyelets so that you can hang your work. Turn your work over, so that you are looking at the back. On the upper inside edge of the frame, screw in an eyelet about 1in (2.5cm) down the side. Place another eyelet on the opposite side of the frame at roughly the same point.

7 Thread a length of wool through the eyelets and tie in a knot. You will now be able to hang your work. Repeat Steps 1–7 to make the other two canvases.

FOR THE SUPER CLEVER PEOPLE

TRICKIER
PROJECTS

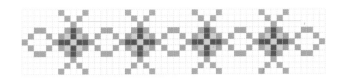

# WATCH STRAP

THIS IS PROBABLY ONE OF THE MOST FIDDLY PROJECTS IN THIS BOOK, BUT I THINK THE RESULTS ARE WORTH IT. I BOUGHT THE WATCH FACE AND BUCKLE ON EBAY. YOU COULD JUST AS EASILY USE THE PARTS FROM AN OLD WATCH, BUT THE IMPORTANT THING IS TO FIND A WATCH WITH A BAR ON EITHER SIDE OF THE FACE TO ATTACH YOUR AIDA STRAPS TO.

On 14-count aida my Navajo-style design (see chart on page 26) is about ¾in (2cm) wide, which makes it a perfect fit for the watch I chose. Sketch your design of choice on graph paper (see pages 145–9) to see which scale would best fit the width of your bars, and select your aida size accordingly.

It is a good idea to choose a design that has lots of gaps and spaces in it, as you will be making small holes down the centre of your strap for the buckle to sit in. The Navajo-style design I have used is perfect for this, as there are evenly spaced gaps running down the centre of the pattern.

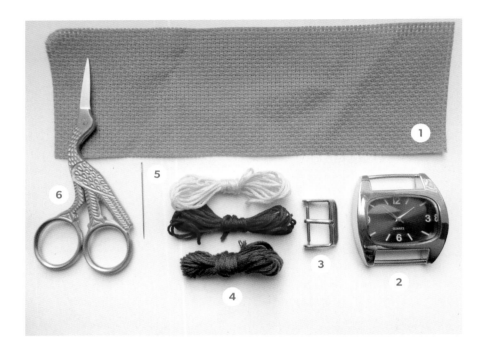

## you will need

1. Aida – enough to make 2 strips at least 2½ x 8in (6 x 20cm) – see advice on measurement in 'Tip' below – and a scrap 2½ x 2¾in (6 x 7cm)

2. Watch face with a bar at each side

3. Buckle

4. Embroidery thread

5. Needle

6. Sharp-pointed scissors

Tip To figure out the exact length of aida you'll need, measure the circumference of your wrist, divide by two and add at least ¾in (2cm) to each strip, as you will need to allow extra to fold over the watch bars or to add your buckle to later on. For the width, allow approximately three times the width of your watch bars.

1 Take your strips of aida and fold them in half lengthways. Make a crease so that you can find the centre point for your design. Work your chosen design (see pages 26–47 for suggestions) so that it runs approx. 5½in (14cm) down the length of each strip, leaving a little spare aida at each end. Fold each long side of the strip over to the wrong side along the top and bottom edges of the cross stitch, creasing the aida firmly. Check that the folded fabric will fit the watch bars.

2 On the reverse, work little straight stitches down the side, using the holes in the aida as a guide to keep the stitches straight and even in size.

1

2

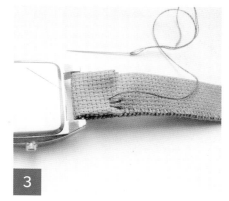

3

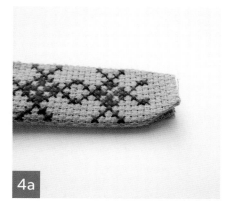

4a

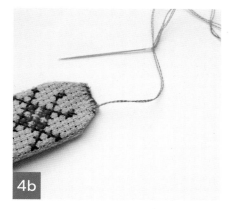

4b

Tip The bars at either side of my watch face are about ¾in (2cm) wide – anything less and the cross-stitch design would have to be very small. The wider it is, the more space and freedom you have to create your design.

3 Thread one strip through the bottom bar of your watch, fold over about ¾in (2cm) of the unstitched aida, and stitch in place as you did with the seam.

4 You will need to taper the other end of this strap, so that it can slip through the buckle more easily when worn. To do this, poke the sides of your strap inside a little and crease firmly, so that they slope inwards (4a). Stitch in place with little straight stitches (4b).

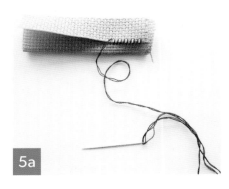

5a

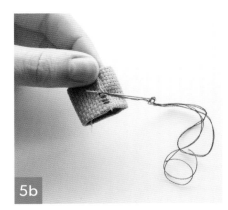

5b

6

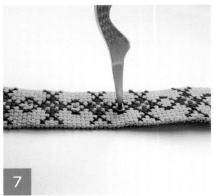

7

5 Now make a small band to keep the strap in place when worn. Take a strip of aida measuring 2¼ x 2½in (6 x 7cm), fold the long sides in, leaving a strip ¾in (2cm) wide. Stitch up the seam as you did for the straps (5a). Fold the strip around the strap and stitch the ends together (5b). Thread this loop onto the remaining strap.

6 Thread one end of the remaining strap through the top bar of the watch and stitch in place, as before. Now decide how long this strap needs to be. I chose to place my buckle about 4in (10cm) down, again leaving ¾in (2cm) at the end to fold over and stitch in place. Slide the buckle onto the end to see where it will sit, and push in the sides of the strap to taper it slightly. With a pair of scissors, push a small hole through the strap and push the tongue of the buckle through it. Now, fold the end of the strap over the bar of the buckle and stitch it in place.

7 You will need to make some evenly spaced holes down the middle of the strap on the bottom of the watch, where the buckle can sit when worn. Use the tips of your scissors to make these holes, gently pushing through the strap and placing them in the gaps of the design where there are no stitches. There is no need to be too vigorous as you do not want to tear the aida; you just want to make small holes for the tongue of your buckle to fit through.

HAVING A
CRAFTY
TIME

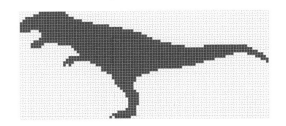

# TOTE BAG

THE AIM OF THIS PROJECT IS TO INTRODUCE YOU TO THE WONDERFUL INVENTION THAT IS WATER-SOLUBLE CANVAS; IT ALLOWS YOU TO WORK IN CROSS STITCH ON FABRICS THAT DON'T HAVE THE EVENWEAVE MARKINGS AND THEN SIMPLY WASHES AWAY, LEAVING YOUR PERFECTLY NEAT STITCHES.

Tote bags are very popular, and it's fun to have a selection to choose from. For this bag, I chose two pieces of fabric that complement each other: a printed piece for the outer part of the bag and a matching plain colour for the lining. I based the size of this tote on bags that I own already, but you can make it any size you wish.

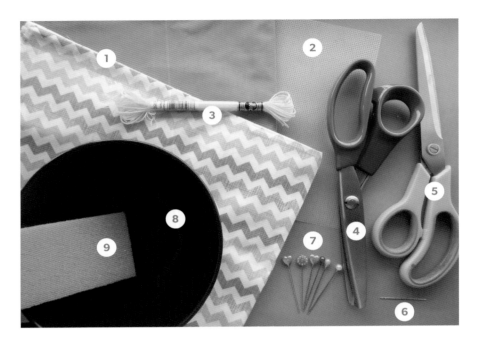

1  Cotton fabric – printed for outer bag and plain for lining. See 'Tip' below for advice on measurements

2  Water-soluble canvas

3  Embroidery thread

4  Pinking shears

5  Fabric scissors (and little sewing scissors to snip your threads if you find these easier)

6  Needle

7  Pins

8  Bowl for hot soapy water

9  Clean cloth or sponge

Tip I measured tote bags that I already own to work out how much fabric I would need. Measure the height of the bag, double it, then add 2in (5cm) top and bottom for hems and seam allowances. Measure the width and add an extra 1in (2.5cm) at each side. Cut your outer and lining fabrics to the same size.

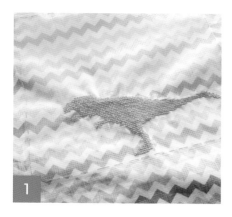

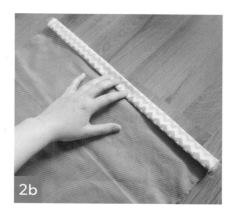

1 Cut a piece of water-soluble canvas and tack it in place on the front of the bag, where you would like your cross-stitch design to go. Work your design onto the canvas. Snip away the tacking stitches and all the excess canvas from around the design. Following the manufacturer's instructions, soak the canvas in hot, soapy water. Dab the area lightly with a clean cloth or sponge. The canvas will start to feel soft and rubbery and will gradually disappear; it will take up to 10 minutes to wash away completely. When it no longer feels sticky, rinse with fresh, cool water and leave the fabric to dry.

2 Place the outer and lining fabrics together, with the cross-stitch design right side down and the lining right side up on top. Fold over the top 1in (2.5cm) of the two pieces of fabric together (2a), then repeat so that you have a double fold (2b).

3 Press firmly along the fold and pin in place. Repeat with the other end of the fabric and fold in half to check that both sides match up nicely.

4 Using either a coordinating thread or a contrasting colour of your choice, use small running stitches to sew the hems in place. Remove the pins.

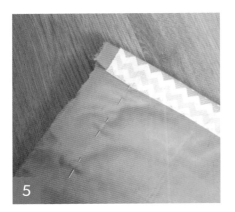

5

6a

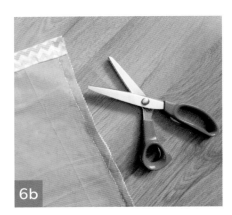

6b

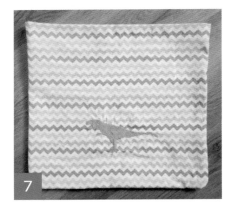

7

5 With the lining on the outside, fold the 'bag' in half and pin up the sides about 1in (2.5cm) in from the edges.

6 Work small running stitches (see page 18) up each side, then remove the pins. With a pair of scissors, snip off the corners from the bottom of the bag (6a). This will help you create nice pointed corners when your bag is finished. Using pinking shears, snip away any excess fabric from each side (6b).

Tip Make sure your stitches are nice and close together and of equal length, but do not worry too much about how they look otherwise, as they will not be seen from the outside when your bag is complete.

7 Turn the bag the right side out and, using your fingers or the tips of your scissors, push the bottom corners into nice points. Press with an iron.

8 Decide how wide you want the straps to be and cut two strips of fabric three times that width and 31½in (80cm) long. Fold one long edge of each strip in by one-third of the strip's width (8a), then fold the other long edge in by the same amount (8b). Press firmly along the folds and pin in place (8c).

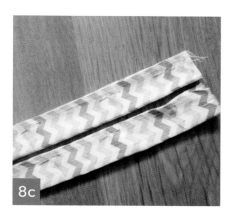

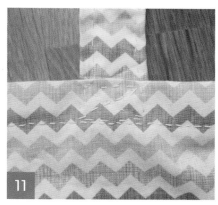

9 Along each strap, run two rows of running stitches. One row will be to hold the seam in place, the other will be purely decorative.

10 Take the body of your bag, and decide where you would like your straps to be positioned. Ensure each strap matches and that neither is twisted. Once you are happy with the position of each, pin in place, carefully tucking under the raw edge of each strap.

11 Using the same thread as for the other seams, stitch each strap in place. Work a little 'box' shape with an 'X' across the middle, as pictured. This will ensure it is firmly held on. Remove the pins as you go. Your bag is now ready to use!

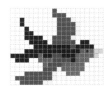

# CUSTOMIZED SHOES

XXXXXXXXXXXXXXXXXXXXXXXXXXXXXXXXXXXXXXXXXXXXXXXXXXXXXXXXXXXXXXXXXXXXX

IT IS VERY COMMON FOR SHOES TO BE CUSTOMIZED WITH FABRIC PENS AND PAINTS, BUT THE BEAUTY OF USING STITCHING IS THAT YOUR DESIGN WILL NOT WASH AWAY WHEN YOU HAVE TO WALK HOME IN THE RAIN! I CHOSE A PLAIN, INEXPENSIVE PAIR OF BLACK COTTON PUMPS TO MAKE MY COLOURFUL SWALLOW MOTIF REALLY 'POP'.

First, look for shoes that are made from a thin cotton material to make sewing easier. Then decide where you want the cross-stitch motif to go on your shoe, and which pattern you want to use. I used the swallows design on page 44 and placed it at one side of each shoe, as it is much easier to work here.

Before you start, make sure you can fit your hand into the end of the shoe with enough space to move a needle freely. Try removing the laces to free up some more room – and do not work too close to the toe, as space here is really tight. If you want to work the toe end, it may be easier to choose a pair of espadrilles or ballet pumps to work on, as these have more space in the toe area.

## you will need

1. Fabric shoes
2. Embroidery thread
3. Needle (strong and sharp!)
4. Scissors
5. Water-soluble canvas
6. Bowl for hot soapy water
7. Clean cloth or sponge

Tip Be inventive: as an extra touch, why not swap the laces for a pair in a contrasting colour?

1 Roughly cut a piece of water-soluble canvas that is big enough to cover the area you will be working on. Thread a needle with cotton thread or a single strand of embroidery thread and roughly tack around the edge of the canvas to hold it in place. As the shoes have a rounded edge, it will be very hard to work your pattern in a precise straight line, but you can use the edges of the pumps as a rough guide when positioning the canvas.

2 Once you are confident the canvas is positioned how you want it to be, so that the evenweave markings are in place, stitch your chosen cross-stitch motif.

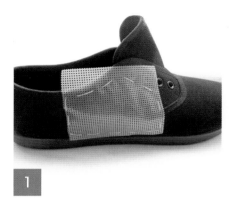

1

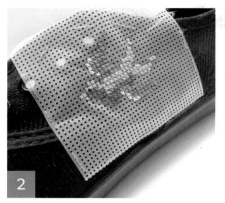

2

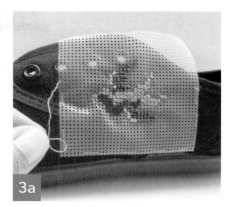

3a

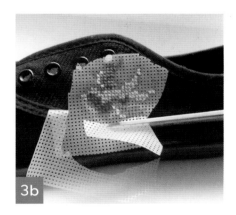

3b

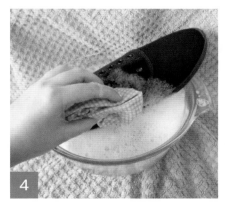

4

5

3 Carefully remove the tacking stitches (3a) and, if necessary, trim away any unused canvas around the edges of your design (3b). You do not have to cut the canvas away neatly: you're only doing this so that there is less to dissolve away.

4 Following the manufacturer's instructions, soak the canvas in hot, soapy water and gently rub over the stitches using your hands and your cloth or sponge. The canvas will start to feel soft and rubbery and gradually it will disappear. This may take a few minutes, as on the Tote Bag project (page 120). When it no longer feels sticky, rinse with cool clean water.

5 You should now have one very soggy shoe. Repeat the process for the other shoe and, when all the canvas has been washed away, leave your shoes to air dry on a towel. Put on your favourite outfit and add your new pumps as a finishing touch!

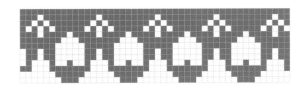

# CUSTOMIZED CLOTHING

THIS PROJECT FOLLOWS THE SAME METHOD AS THE
CUSTOMIZED SHOES ON PAGE 126, BUT SHOWS HOW
YOU CAN USE IT TO REVAMP OTHER ITEMS OF CLOTHING.
I CHOSE THE 'LACE' DESIGN FROM THE BORDERS PATTERNS
ON PAGE 32 TO UPDATE AN OLD DENIM SHIRT. I DECIDED
IT WOULD LOOK GOOD RUNNING ALONG THE STRAIGHT
LINE OF THE SEAM ON THE SHOULDERS, AND WENT FOR
A DEEP BERRY-RED SHADE OF THREAD FOR A SUBTLE EFFECT.

Preparation is key for this project. First you will need to decide on the type of design you want to stitch (take a look at the charts on pages 26–47 for suggestions) and where you want it to go on the item of clothing you have chosen. It's then a good idea to draw the design onto a piece of graph paper (see page 22) to the same scale as the water-soluble canvas you have. This will give you an idea of how big the design will be when stitched, and therefore whether it will fit into the area on your clothing that you want it to. It may take a few attempts, especially if you've chosen quite an ambitious design, but persevere, because the end result will be worth it – a one-off item of clothing!

## you will need

1. Item of clothing to customize
2. Embroidery thread
3. Water-soluble canvas
4. Needle
5. Pins
6. Scissors
7. Bowl for hot soapy water
8. Clean cloth or sponge

Tip Check the care instructions on the clothing first, as you will have to hand wash the area of stitching in hot, soapy water. If the colours are likely to run because it is new, or if the fabric is likely to shrink, wash and dry it before you work your cross-stitch motif. Use the kind of mild soap you would use to wash your dishes with – avoid any strong detergents.

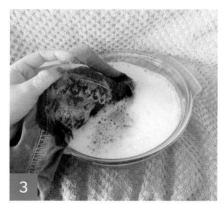

1 Cut a piece of water-soluble canvas big enough to cover the area you will be working on and pin it in place (1a). Once you are happy with the positioning, use some spare embroidery thread or cotton to tack it in place, then remove the pins (1b); your stitches do need not be neat, as they will be removed when you have finished.

2 Now work your cross-stitch motif on the water-soluble canvas in the same way that you would on aida. It is impossible for it to sit perfectly flat and taut against your clothing, but your stitches will still look neat. When you have completed your design, unpick the tacking stitches (2a) and trim off any excess water-soluble canvas (2b).

3 Fill a bowl with hot, soapy water. Dunk the cross-stitched area into the bowl and rub over the stitches gently with your hands. You can also use a clean cloth or sponge, but do not rub hard as you don't want to damage your stitching. The canvas will start to feel soft and rubbery and after 5–10 minutes it will have disappeared. Rinse with clean water and leave to dry.

# HANDKERCHIEF OR HEADSCARF

COTTON HANDKERCHIEFS MAY BE CONSIDERED A LITTLE OLD-FASHIONED, BUT FOR THE ENVIRONMENTALLY CONSCIOUS THEY ARE ALSO RE-USEABLE. HANKIES ARE USED TO SEND SIGNALS, TO BUFF SHOES, TO CARRY YOUR SANDWICHES IN A KNAPSACK LIKE DICK WHITTINGTON – THINK ABOUT IT, THEY'RE PRETTY COOL!

Over the page, I have provided the measurements for a lady's handkerchief and a gentleman's, plus the dimensions for turning the project into a headscarf. You can either use a matching thread for the hems, so that the stitches will not be seen, or (as I have done) a contrasting colour to make the stitches more of a feature. Play around with different fabric options and colour schemes, too. I have chosen quite a muted fabric so that the butterfly motif catches the eye, but an item like a handkerchief or headscarf can be as bold and bright as you like.

# you will need

1. Cotton fabric
2. Embroidery thread
3. Pins
4. Water-soluble canvas
5. Needle
6. Scissors
7. Bowl for hot soapy water
8. Clean cloth or sponge

Tip As with most of the projects in this book, you can make this to any size you like, but here are some size guidelines:

Woman's handkerchief:
10 x 10in (25 x 25cm)
Gentleman's handkerchief:
15 x 15in (30 x 30cm)
Headscarf:
20 x 20in (50 x 50cm)

1 The first thing you need to do is give your handkerchief or scarf nice edges, so that it will not fray. Take the first edge and fold over a very small amount twice, so that any frayed edges are completely hidden underneath. Work small running stitches (see page 18) along the entire length of this side. When you get to the end of this side, fold over the next side in the same way and continue.

2 Now decide where you would like to stitch your motif. Cut a piece of water-soluble canvas to cover this area, and tack it in place. The tacking stitches can be as messy as you like, as they will be removed when you have finished your design.

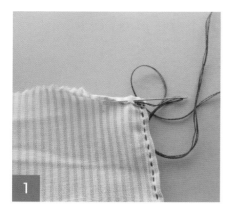
1

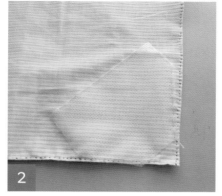
2

3

4a

4b

5

3 Stitch your chosen motif (see charts on pages 26–47 for suggestions). Traditionally, people stitched their initials into the corner of their hankie. I opted for a butterfly, but you can choose whatever you fancy.

4 When you have completed your design, remove the tacking stitches (4a) and cut away any excess water-soluble canvas around your design (4b).

5 Following the manufacturer's instructions, soak the fabric in hot, soapy water and dab at the stitched motif gently with a clean cloth or sponge. The water-soluble canvas will start to go rubbery as it dissolves; it will take up to 10 minutes to wash away completely and you will know it is ready when it no longer feels sticky. Rinse under cool water, squeeze gently and leave to dry. Press.

Tip If you run out of thread while working the running stitches in Step 1, hide the thread under the folded hem, snip it away, and insert a fresh piece with its loose end (or knot, if you choose to use one) hidden under the hem. The corners of the hankie will take care of themselves, but use your needle or a discreet stitch or two to tidy up any loose ends as you go.

# PETER PAN COLLAR

PETER PAN COLLARS ARE PERFECT FOR WEARING OVER AN OTHERWISE PLAIN AND BORING T-SHIRT TO MAKE IT LOOK TEN TIMES MORE FANCY. THIS PROJECT DEMONSTRATES A BASIC METHOD FOR MAKING YOUR OWN, BUT THERE ARE SO MANY WAYS YOU COULD ELABORATE ON IT.

You could use printed cotton fabric, or perhaps two contrasting fabrics to form the top and bottom of your collar. You could even devise your own template, using mine as a starting point – maybe you could make a collar with pointy edges or a pretty scalloped edge around the bottom? Instead of a ribbon as a tie at the front, why not add your own cross-stitched button? The possibilities are endless! Have fun with it.

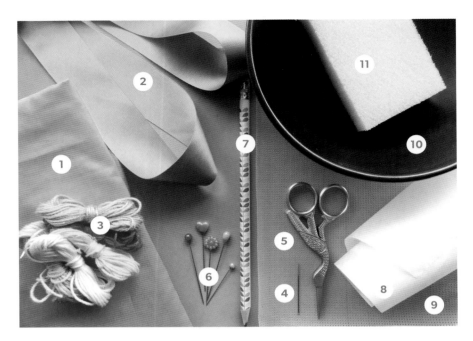

## you will need

1. Cotton fabric, approx. 23½ x 15½in (60 x 40cm)

2. 20in (50cm) ribbon, 1in (2.5cm) wide

3. Embroidery thread

4. Needle

5. Scissors

6. Pins

7. Pencil

8. Tracing paper

9. Water-soluble canvas

10. Bowl for hot soapy water

11. Clean cloth or sponge

Optional: dressmaker's chalk or washable fabric pen

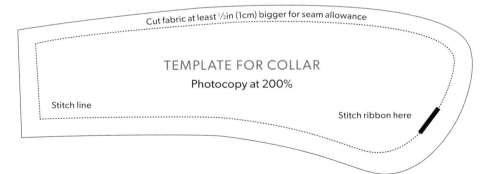

Cut fabric at least ½in (1cm) bigger for seam allowance

TEMPLATE FOR COLLAR
Photocopy at 200%

Stitch line

Stitch ribbon here

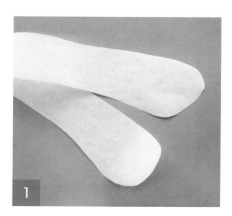

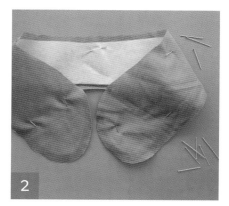

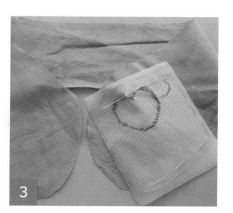

1 Photocopy the template on the facing page at 200%, then trace it twice onto tracing paper. Cut and stick the thin ends together to make one complete collar. Pin to a new sheet of tracing paper, draw around the outside, and cut out, so you have one single pattern piece.

2 Place the pattern on your chosen fabric and pin in place. Using your pencil, draw around the edge and cut out, leaving at least ½in (1.25cm) around the edge for the seam allowance. Repeat so that you have two collar pieces.

Tip Your pencil marks in Step 2 will not be seen on the finished piece, but if you would prefer to use dressmaker's chalk or a washable fabric marker pen instead, then do so.

3 Decide where you would like your stitched design to go. (See charts on pages 26–47 for design suggestions.) I decided I wanted two motifs, one at each side of the front of my collar. Cut pieces of water-soluble canvas to fit the area you want to place your design in. I counted the number of squares on the canvas going across and up, to give me a rough idea of how big my design could be. Tack the canvas in place; the tacking stitches can be as messy as you like, as they will be removed shortly. Work your cross-stitch designs.

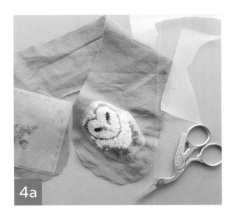

4a

4b

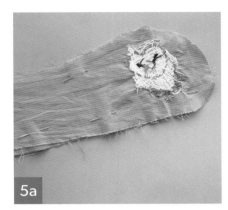

5a

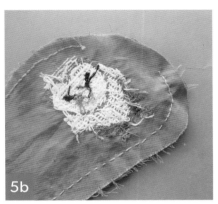

5b

6

4 Once complete, remove the tacking stitches and cut away any excess canvas (4a). Following the manufacturer's instructions, soak the collar in hot, soapy water and dab gently with a sponge until all the water-soluble canvas has gone (4b). It will start to feel rubbery and take up to 10 minutes to dissolve completely. You will know it has dissolved when it no longer feels sticky. Rinse in cool water, squeeze away any excess water and leave to dry.

5 Pin the two collar pieces right sides together (5a). Work a running stitch (see page 18) around the edge, stitching about ½in (1.25cm) from the edge and leaving a gap at the top of each side of the collar front, as marked on the template (5b); these gaps are where you will stitch your ribbon to tie the collar at the front.

6 Turn the collar right side through one of the gaps at the front.

Tip To prevent the ends of the ribbons from fraying after you have cut the tips in Step 7, you could add a small amount of clear all-purpose glue or nail varnish to the edges.

YOU COULD EXPERIMENT
WITH ADAPTING THE COLLAR
TEMPLATE TO MAKE YOUR
OWN UNIQUE COLLAR SHAPES
– MAKE THE ENDS OF THE
COLLAR POINTED, OR GIVE IT
A SCALLOPED EDGE.

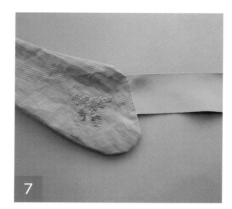

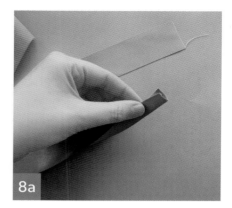

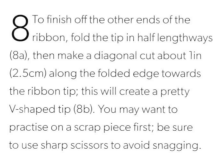

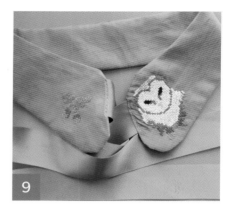

7 Cut your length of ribbon in half. Insert one end of ribbon into one of the gaps you left at the front of the collar, turn the raw edges of the gap under and pin in place. Using either a matching or contrasting colour of thread, stitch the ribbon in place with small running stitches, then remove the pin. Repeat on the other side of the collar.

8 To finish off the other ends of the ribbon, fold the tip in half lengthways (8a), then make a diagonal cut about 1in (2.5cm) along the folded edge towards the ribbon tip; this will create a pretty V-shaped tip (8b). You may want to practise on a scrap piece first; be sure to use sharp scissors to avoid snagging.

9 Press gently: you now have a pretty collar ready to wear.

*In the common parlance of 1950s America,*

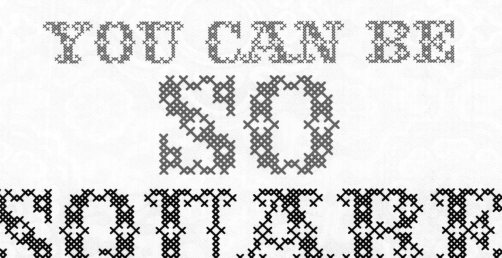

YOU CAN BE
SO
SQUARE

GRID: aida count 12in (30.5cm)

GRID: aida count 14in (35.5cm)

# Resources

IF YOU'VE BEEN BITTEN BY THE CROSS-STITCH BUG,
THERE ARE A WHOLE HOST OF ONLINE RESOURCES WHERE
YOU CAN BUY MATERIALS AND EQUIPMENT, PICK UP USEFUL
TECHNICAL TIPS OR SIMPLY GET IN TOUCH WITH OTHER
PEOPLE WHO SHARE YOUR ENTHUSIASM.

## Suppliers

Here are the suppliers I like to use for sourcing aida, embroidery thread and just about everything else I need.

### Anchor and DMC

These are two of the most popular brands when it comes to all your cross-stitch needs. Each has a huge choice of shades of thread as well as more fancy products:
**www.dmccreative.co.uk**
**www.coatscrafts.co.uk**
If you have purchased a shade of floss by Anchor, have used it all up and can no longer find any more, you can use this nifty site to help you convert that specific shade to a matching one by **DMC:**
www.stitchtastic.com/useful/
AnchorToDMC.aspx

### eBay

For anyone who doesn't know, eBay is an online auction site. I often search here for unusual coloured aida that is hard to find on the high street, and large quantities of embroidery floss.
**www.ebay.com**

### Etsy

Etsy is a magnificent online marketplace for all things vintage and handmade.
It is home to my online store and also to thousands of other stores from makers around the globe. As well as handmade items, it is a great source of supplies.
**Spy on my handmade wares here:**
**www.etsy.com/shop/mamagasin**
and lose yourself in Etsy in its full glory here: **www.etsy.com**

### Fred Aldous

Fred Aldous has been in business for over 125 years and I am fortunate enough to live in the same city as its bricks-and-mortar shop, with two huge floors packed full of craft essentials. Take a look around their online shop here:
**www.fredaldous.co.uk**

### Hobbycraft

The majority of craft shops are little independent affairs, but Hobbycraft is sort of like the Big Cheese of craft shops.
**www.hobbycraft.co.uk**

### Willow Fabrics

I like to hit Willow Fabrics as my first port of call for large quantities of aida.
**www.willowfabrics.com**

## Other useful sites

These sites are all cross-stitch mad and a great source of patterns, tips on techniques, supplies and kits.
**www.allcrossstitch.co.uk**
**www.cross-stitching.com**
**www.cross-stitch-centre.co.uk**
**www.sewandso.co.uk**

### The Cross Stitch Guild

The Cross Stitch Guild was formed by well-known designer and author Jane Greenoff and has now become a worldwide organization. Greenoff is a hero of mine as, just like me, she is a self-taught stitcher.
Head here for everything from cross-stitch news to events.
**www.thecrossstitchguild.com**

## Magazines

If the Internet is making you square-eyed, head to your local shop and pick up some of these magazines! Many craft magazines come with free kits to make your own cross-stitch picture, and I am particularly a fan of any craft magazine that has a feature on snooping around makers' studios:

*Making*
www.makingmagazine.com

*Mollie Makes*
www.molliemakes.com

*Cross Stitcher*
www.crossstitcher.themakingspot.com

# About the author

*Sarah Fordham is a Fine Art graduate and cross-stitch fanatic from The Garden of England, also known as Kent. She can usually be found cross stitching on the sofa while watching DVD box sets, surrounded by chocolate wrappers. When she isn't stitching or designing, she can be found working as a window dresser, poring over Jake Gyllenhaal blogs, cooing over puppies and collecting plaid clothing.*

Follow Sarah at:
**www.facebook.com/weheartmagasin**
Twitter: **@magasinxstitch**
Instragram: **magasinxstitch**

# Acknowledgements

High fives to my family, best buds Ferg and Ryan, all at Cath Kidston in Manchester, who I've had the pleasure of working with, Gus The Fox, and all those who have supported my work.

Eternal thanks to all the people who send me amazing custom requests and continue to purchase items from my Etsy shop.

Also, a huge thank you to Etsy for being great and to the team at GMC Publications who made this book possible.

Thank you!

# Index

To place an order, or to request a catalogue, contact:

GMC Publications Ltd, Castle Place, 166 High Street, Lewes, East Sussex, BN7 1XU, United Kingdom

Tel: +44 (0)1273 488005

www.gmcbooks.com